NASHVILLE
The Delaplaine
2016 Long Weekend Guide

Andrew Delaplaine

NO BUSINESS HAS PAID A SINGLE PENNY OR GIVEN *ANYTHING* TO BE INCLUDED IN THIS BOOK.

A list of the author's other travel guides, as well as his political thrillers and titles for children, can be found at the end of this book.

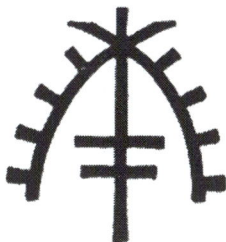

Senior Editors - *Renee & Sophie Delaplaine*
Senior Writer - **James Cubby**

Gramercy Park Press
New York – London - Paris

Please submit corrections, additions or comments to
andrewdelaplaine@mac.com

NASHVILLE
The Delaplaine
2016 Long Weekend Guide

TABLES OF CONTENTS

LONG WEEKEND SERIES

Like you, when I'm heading into a new place, I have bought travel guides and toiled through them hour after hour trying to extract from the book the "essence" of the city or region I was visiting. Sometimes, sadly, I spent more hours reading the book than I did in the town it purported to tell me about. To judge by the size of some of these books, you'd think I was planning on spending my life there, not just a few days.

By including exhaustive detail in their guidebooks, many writers actually end up obscuring the essence of the city they're writing about rather than revealing it.

If you're going to stay two or more weeks in a place, then by all means do your homework. There are hundreds of guides, both in print and online, to assist you.

But if you've only got 3 or 4 days, your needs really are different.

I would want to know:

= **LODGINGS**. What would be the best hotels or B&Bs or inns to choose from? I would want a choice of 4 or 5 places in different budget categories. (For the kid with a backpack will be on a different budget than someone on an expense account. A retired couple will have different wants and needs than a family of four.)

= **RESTAURANTS**. What would be a good selection of restaurants, again within different budget levels, that would represent the area I'm visiting? Again, whether expensive or cheap, which of the thousands of places to eat will give me a feel for the town?

= **ATTRACTIONS.** Of all the attractions and things to do, which are the most important that will leave me with memories that I've really *seen* the place?

= **SHOPPING?** Something different and out of the way reflective of the area. Not the big chains, whether that chain is Tiffany or the Gap. Something local.

Rather than craft a definitive itinerary for you the way many others have done, I've expanded the listings in each section so that you could get a good range of the offerings available—so you can pick and choose among them to craft your own special Long Weekend.

Chapter 1
WHY NASHVILLE?

Every city has its own nickname. (Some even have more than one.) New York is the Big Apple. New Orleans is the Big Easy. Chicago is the City of the Big Shoulders.

Nashville is Music City, pure and simple. When you hear the term Music City, you only think of one town, and that town is Nashville.

While Memphis is a larger city than Nashville, Nashville is the capital of Tennessee. I never actually thought about that till I first arrived here. My initial reaction on hearing that Nashville was the capital of Tennessee was to think how odd that sounded. I'd only thought of Nashville as the "Country Music Capital of the World," which of course it is. Not as the capital of anything else.

Having been raised in South Carolina, I well remember seeing Minnie Pearl on TV in broadcasts from the **Grand Ole Opry**, which has done weekly shows since 1925, making it the longest continuously broadcast radio show in history.

Nashville is not only the center of the country music business, but for Christian music as well.

They city has outgrown its label as a purely "country" town. What makes it particularly unique is that it combines the best elements of a small town (people say "Hello" on the streets, the clerks in the shops are as pleasant as can be) with the sophistication of a big town (the museums are superlative, the galleries cutting edge, the restaurants are world class—repeat the words **Catbird Seat** and **Rolf & Daughters** to me).

The restaurant scene has exploded, and now features some of the most original cooking that stands up to the best that New York has to offer. Just look at what they're doing at the **Catbird Seat.** I find it particularly interesting that Sean Brock, who so successfully opened Husk and McCrady's in Charleston, opted to return to Nashville (where he once worked for 3 years at the Hermitage) with a local version of **Husk**. If Brock's presence doesn't say something about the food scene in Nashville, nothing does.

The bar scene also has greatly expanded, offering much more variety. As for nightlife, there's never been anyplace with so much music going on. Start at the **Bluebird Café** (the location of scenes in ABC's "Nashville" TV show, though they use a set that recreates the site) and then dig deeper.

The formerly down-and-dirty **12 South District** has bounced back big-time with eateries offering sustainable cuisine, trendy shops, a cutting edge atmosphere, making it one of the hotter new areas of town. Meanwhile, in what's now called **SoBro** (meaning that it's directly south of the famous Broadway honky-tonk area), once home to almost nothing, you can experience a whole new neighborhood coming alive as it changes day by day, with famous chefs opening restaurants and craft cocktails being served at new hotspots.

One thing I guarantee: You'll never get Nashville out of your blood.

Chapter 2
WHERE TO STAY

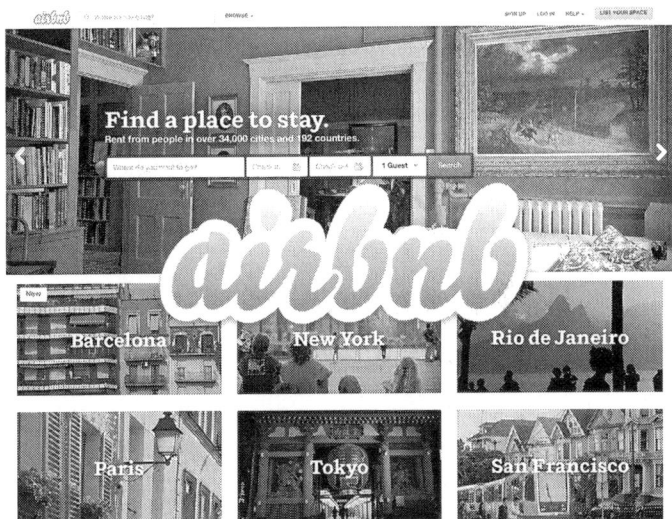

AIRBNB
www.airbnb.com
Book a room or an entire apartment from an individual. You pay
AirBnB and they pay the host after you check in. The good thing
here is that you get to review the host (but the host also gets to
review you after you leave), and this process works to keep both
sides honest.

PRICELINE and HOTWIRE
www.priceline.com
www.hotwire.com
With Priceline, you bid on rooms in the part of the city where
you want to stay, select whatever star levels you want, and
generally can get cheaper rooms. These are usually in hotel
chains, so nothing with too much character. With Hotwire, they
tell you the price of the room. You don't bid on it. You can often

play one site off against the other to get an even cheaper deal. (You don't find out the name of the lodging until you close the deal.)

404 HOTEL
404 12th Ave S, Nashville, 615-251-1404
www.the404nashville.com
Located in the Gulch neighborhood, this unique urban oasis offers five king rooms with a mix of vintage and custom furniture. Amenities include: gourmet pastries delivered from nearby bakery, and in-room refrigerators stocked with complimentary drinks.

THE DRAKE INN
420 Murfreesboro Pike, Nashville, 615-256-7770
www.drakeinnnashville.com
This two-level historic inn features 101 well-appointed guest rooms with modern conveniences. Amenities include: swimming pool, Jacuzzi, cable TVs and free internet access. Conveniently located near Downtown area, Music Row, Country Hall of Fame and other local attractions. While there's no restaurant on site, there are plenty of good ones nearby. Pet-friendly hotel.

GAYLORD OPRYLAND RESORT AND CONVENTION CENTER
2800 Opryland Dr, Nashville, 615-889-1000
www.gaylordhotels.com
This resort and convention center offers 2,881 guest rooms all decorated with a Southern flair. Amenities include: free high-speed Internet access, cable TVs, movie channels, and coffeemakers. This hotel features 9 acres of indoor gardens, cascading waterfalls, an indoor river, and **indoor and outdoor swimming pools, and** a 20,000 square foot spa and fitness center. The resort features an amazing selection of on-site restaurants for the guests dining pleasure. Smoke-free hotel. It's all a little much, but if you're looking for a "one-stop shop" kind of place to stay, this would be the place.

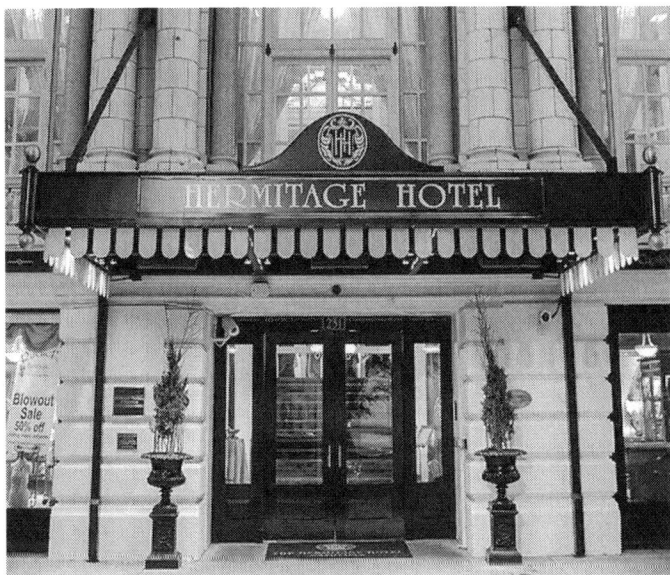

THE HERMITAGE HOTEL
231 Sixth Ave N, Nashville, 615-244-3121
www.thehermitagehotel.com
NEIGHBORHOOD: Downtown

Oh, what a lovely hotel. It looks like it belongs in New York City when you first pull up to it, with its majestic Beaux-Arts stone façade, the high arched windows rising from the second floor, each arch framed by double Corinthian columns. But as soon as you get out of your cab, you'll realize you're not in New York because of the Southern hospitality. It starts right with the doorman. (Lots of musicians and people in the music industry stay here.) It's been one of the more elegant places to stay in Nashville since it opened in 1910. You'll love the ornate lobby ceiling with its soaring coffered arches, the plush chairs gathered around the fireplace. When the place opened, it had 250 rooms. But the remodeling over the years has brought the count down to 122, with renovations updating the lodgings and enlarging the rooms to between 500 and 650 square feet (larger than my first apartment in New York). From lots of the rooms you can get superlative views of Downtown as well as the State Capitol. Big marble bathrooms with double vanities; soaking tubs; separate shower; down-filled duvets; flat screen TVs, free Internet and lots of other amenities. 24-hour room service. Spa Services: massages, wraps, scrub treatments and much more. Pet friendly. Business center including secretarial services. The on-site restaurant is the **Capitol Grille**, which is very, very good, serving vegetables grown and beef raised from farms nearby. The only hotel in Tennessee that carries both the Forbes Five Star and AAA Five diamond ratings. Also has the **Oak Bar**, a great place for a meeting or even a romantic drink before or after dinner. (Tip: Has a good happy hour that attracts a lot of locals, 4:30 to 6:30.)

HILTON NASHVILLE DOWNTOWN   July 1-5, 2016
121 4th Ave S, Nashville, 615-620-1000
http://www3.hilton.com/en/hotels/tennessee/hilton-nashville-downtown-BNANSHF/index.html
NEIGHBORHOOD: Downtown
This all-suite hotel has an AAA Four-Diamond rating. Has undergone serious renovations to its lobby and some 300 suites. Has the faceless look of a typical businessman's hotel on the

outside, but it's nice enough inside, with a little "creek" running through the atrium-style lobby. The rooms are spic-and-span, modern, and the hotel has all the amenities (fitness room, business center) you expect at a Hilton property. Also has **Parkview Café** in the lobby, which makes a good spot for a quick (if uninspired) lunch, as well as the **Sportsgrille**, a good place to drink some beer and catch the game on one of their TVs. **The Palm Steakhouse** is worth coming to even if you're not staying here. Nothing run-of-the-mill about this place.)

HOMEWOOD SUITES
706 Church St, Nashville, 615-742-5550
www.homewood.hilton.com/Nashville
NEIGHBORHOOD: Downtown
If you're looking for an "extended stay" lodging in Downtown, Homewood Suites, located in the historic Doctor's Building, is a good bet. (If you want a little more upscale property with suites only, go to the **Hilton**—see above.) But it's also good for a Long Weekend. They only offer suites, and they come with full kitchens, free Internet and free hot breakfast.

HOTEL INDIGO

301 Union St, Nashville, 888-897-0095
http://www.ihg.com/hotelindigo/hotels/us/en/nashville/bnaus/hot
eldetail/directions
NEIGHBORHOOD: Downtown
Located in a majestic building that used to house the Nashville
Trust back in the 1920s. Not quite in the heart of Downtown, but
just a few blocks away. The lobby has a "printer's theme,"
because the hotel is close to Printer's Row. This is not a luxury
hotel, but it's still good, with a location in an historic building, a
contemporary renovation that really works, an excellent on-site
restaurant, the **District Bar & Kitchen**, live music downstairs
off the lobby. The prices here can be very attractive, so check
them out.

HUTTON HOTEL

1808 W End St, Nashville, 615-340-9333
www.huttonhotel.com
NEIGHBORHOOD: West End
It's not that impressive from the outside, but once you're inside,
it's a completely different story. I love the 1950s styled stairs in
the lobby. You almost expect Doris Day and Rock Hudson to
walk down them, squabbling. High-end 4-Star hotel that's proud
of its "green" reputation. They use highly renewable bamboo
flooring and furnishings; card readers that turn out the lights

when you leave the room—the rooms, by the way, are notably spacious; LED lighting throughout the hotel; dual flush toilets, etc. In their excellent on-site **1808 Grille**, reclaimed wood is used in the décor (to very great advantage, I might add). The 250 room and 50 suites are super contemporary in design, with lots of high-tech amenities; coffee maker in the room; hair dryers; media hubs; plush robes and the like. 24-hour room service from the 1808 Grille.

LOEWS VANDERBILT HOTEL
2100 W End Ave, Nashville, 615-320-1700
www.loewshotels.com/vanderbilt
NEIGHBORHOOD: West End
Right across from Vanderbilt U, this is a AAA Four Diamond property, and has been for decades. It's big, with 340 rooms, 14 very fine suites. The list of amenities goes on and on. Stay on the Club Level and get access to their 2-story Concierge Lounge on the top two floors, with extras like expanded Continental breakfast (with egg), fresh fruits, pastries, etc. you can get coffee, tea and snacks all day, and free beer and wine and canapés at cocktail hour. There's also an excellent view of the university from these high floors. The hotel has a fine restaurant on site as well, **Mason's**, which serves a kind of "Southern Brasserie" cuisine, which take traditionally French dishes and

gives them a Southern twist. The bar here has a lively scene as well.

MILLENIUM MAXWELL HOUSE HOTEL
2025 Rosa L Parks Blvd, Nashville, 615-259-4343
www.milleniumhotels.com
This property has a "Country Music" theme, so if you're into country music (and why else would you come to Nashville if you weren't?), this makes an excellent choice.

MUSIC CITY HOSTEL
1809 Patterson St, Nashville, 615-692-1277
www.musiccityhostel.com
This budget alternative offers shared dorm rooms as well as private rooms.

NASHVILLE FARM STAY
8528 Lewis Rd, Bellevue, 615-425-3616
www.nashvillefarmstay.com
Located on 6 acres and surrounded by beautiful oak and maple trees, this newly renovated 3-bedroom home offers a great alternative to hotels out in rural Bellevue. The home is completely furnished and features a front screened-in porch and a backyard with a full patio. Located one mile from the **Natchez Trace Parkway**, this urban retreat is also close to eateries like the legendary **Loveless Café**.

SCARRITT-BENNET CENTER
1008 19th Ave S, Nashville, 615-340-7500
www.scarrittbennett.org
This is another budget property that offers private rooms, but you have to share a bathroom. Close to Vanderbilt and Music Row.

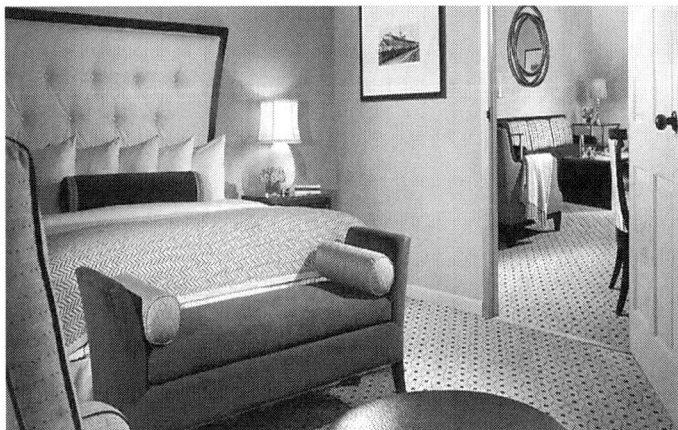

THE UNION STATION HOTEL
1001 Broadway, 615-726-1001
www.unionstationhotelnashville.com
Formerly a railroad station, this hidden gem is breathtaking from the moment you enter the lobby with its 65-foot barrel-vaulted ceiling. The recently renovated hotel offers 125 guest rooms and 12 deluxe suites. Amenities include: LCD flat screen TVs, high-speed wireless Internet access, Pay-Per-View and Web TV, coffeemaker with coffee, and free daily newspaper. On-site cocktails and dining is available at the **Prime 108 Lounge** and **Prime 108 Restaurant**. Conveniently located near attractions like Ryman Auditorium and LP Field. Smoke-free hotel.

Chapter 3
WHERE TO EAT

EatWith
www.eatwith.com
For $35 (and up) you can attend cooking classes or enjoy a dining experience in someone's home. This company connects visitors and residents together (like AirBnb or Paypal) in over 30 countries. So if you're in Brazil and want a home-cooked meal, check it out. Or anywhere else in the world. Expect an intimate experience, as most groups are VERY small. EatWith says that some 60% of their clients stay in touch with either their hosts or co-attendees of the class or meal.

12 SOUTH TAPROOM AND GRILL
2318 12th Ave S, Nashville, 615-463-7552
www.12southtaproom.com
CUISINE: American (New)
DRINKS: Beer & Wine
SERVING: Lunch, Dinner, Closed Sunday
PRICE RANGE: $$
NEIGHBORHOOD: Belmont/Hillsboro

This is a popular spot for locals serving great food and cocktails. Their beer list is extensive, and I'd guess they have the biggest selection representing Nashville's small-batch breweries. The grill's menu includes everything from burgers to tacos, sandwiches and burritos. Menu favorites include: Grilled Salmon and the Garlic Stuffed Roasted Pork Loin. Vegetarian options available.

404 KITCHEN
404 12th Ave S, Nashville, 615-251-1404
www.the404nashville.com
CUISINE: American
DRINKS: Full Bar
SERVING: Dinner, Closed Sun & Mon
PRICE RANGE: $$$
NEIGHBORHOOD: Downtown; Gulch
Located next to the **Station Inn** in a former shipping container (that's right, a real shipping container), this very small eatery (about 40 seats) offers a menu of modern classic European cuisine. Menu favorites include: Glendale Farms Chicken leg confit and Peach and Pork Ragout. The impressive Chef Matt Bolus runs the place, which features indoor and outdoor dining.

1808 GILLE
HUTTON HOTEL
1808 W End St, Nashville, 615-340-9333
www.huttonhotel.com
CUISINE: American
DRINKS: Full Bar
SERVING: Breakfast (from 6:30), Lunch & Dinner daily;
Brunch on weekends from 10:30
PRICE RANGE: $$$
NEIGHBORHOOD: West End
In keeping with the trendy contemporary design of the hotel in
which it's situated, the 1808 Grille is similarly upbeat, modern,
sleek and hip. Boxed-in beige banquettes fill the room, which
has an odd sculpture that looks like big boxes stacked unevenly
atop one another as they climb to the high ceiling. The seasonal
menu here is excellent. Expect items like crispy calamari with
Italian sausage, smoked mussels, polenta croutons; warm duck
salad; butternut squash bisque; quail with parsnip hash (which is
so tasty I ordered an extra side of it).

ARNOLD'S COUNTRY KITCHEN
605 8th Ave S, Nashville, 615-256-4455
No Website
CUISINE: Southern
DRINKS: No Booze
SERVING: Lunch, Closed Sat & Sun
PRICE RANGE: $
NEIGHBORHOOD: Downtown
This place is always busy so expect a line. The menu changes daily with favorites like Chicken and Dumplings, Meatloaf, and BBQ Chicken and Catfish. Here you'll find authentic Southern dishes served in a "meat plus three" style (that's meat plus three sides for all you non-Southerners). You will dine family-style.

BELLA NASHVILLE
Farmers Market
900 Rosa L. Parks Blvd, Nashville, 615-457-3863
www.bellanashville.com
CUISINE: Pizza
DRINKS: No Booze
SERVING: Lunch
PRICE RANGE: $
NEIGHBORHOOD: Downtown

Here you'll find specialty pizzas made to order and creative sandwiches. Menu favorites include: Peaches N' Cream Pizza and Margherita pizza. Nice selection of herbal teas.

CAPITOL GRILLE
THE HERMITAGE HOTEL
231 Sixth Ave N, Nashville, 615-345-7116
www.thehermitagehotel.com
CUISINE: American
DRINKS: Full Bar
SERVING: Breakfast (from 6:30), Lunch & Dinner daily
PRICE RANGE: $$$$
NEIGHBORHOOD: Downtown
As I said above in the listing for the hotel where this dark-ceilinged dining room is housed, the Chef, Tyler Brown, who also owns the farm, grows the vegetables served here. The beef? Raised by Double H Farms just outside town, owned by the Heritage Hotel. Tyler changes his menus with the seasons to reflect what he can get fresh. Between the high arches are murals depicting Nashville scenes. House-cured country ham chowder; venison loin served with apples and parsnips; short rib pot roast; Brussels sprouts with bacon and brown sugar (I've never had Brussels sprouts served like this—just delicious); for dessert try the peanut butter chocolate chess pie served with banana ice

cream and peanut brittle. Oh, and the charming **Oak Bar** located here, always an excellent choice for a drink.

CATBIRD SEAT
1711 Division St, Nashville, 615-810-8200
www.thecatbirdseatrestaurant.com
CUISINE: American
DRINKS: Full bar; $30 corkage fee (ouch!) if you bring your own wine
SERVING: Dinner Wednesday-Sunday; closed Monday & Tuesday; reservations from 5:30; last reservations at 9:15
PRICE RANGE: $$$$
They have a couple of booths against the wall, but most people want one of the 20 seats at the square-shaped counter surrounding the open kitchen, where the chef & his team make your multi-course meal (over $100 per person, but it includes wine and booze, so it's not as expensive as it sounds) while you watch. Whichever chef makes the course will deliver it to you personally so you can ask questions. There's no menu and you won't be able to find out what you're eating till you get there. But this is one of the hottest tickets in Nashville. It's next to the **Patterson House.** The food is exquisite, and if you can bear up to 3 hours to get through the experience, you will be handsomely

rewarded. Expect items like: aged roasted duck; pork sandwich; duck breast with strawberries & almonds; hot & spicy chicken skins; crisp country ham; oyster with seaweed; snapper poached with chorizo; sea urchin with beets; charcoal grilled turbot. The desserts are standouts.

You have to reserve on their web site. Reservation dates open up 30 days in advance. If you cancel, you have to do so 7 days before your reservation or pay a $75 fee. Walk-ins are not accepted.

CITY HOUSE
1222 4th Ave N, Nashville, 615-736-5838
www.cityhousenashville.com
CUISINE: Italian
DRINKS; Full Bar
SERVING: Dinner
PRICE RANGE: $$$
NEIGHBORHOOD: Germantown
Chef Tandy Wilson has an Italian menu with a lot of Southern twists. He believes in the "snout to tail" approach when it comes to animals, and that's why he gets in whole pigs and uses every bit of them. You'll find his house-cured sausage in a pasta dish

and then find ham from the pig's belly on one of his pizzas (the pizzas are unlike any you've ever had). Based on what I've said so far, you'll want to focus on the charcuterie items here in his big open room with brick walls that formerly was a sculptor's studio.

CRYING WOLF
823 Woodland St, Nashville, 615-953-6715
www.thecryingwolf.com
CUISINE: Burgers
DRINKS: Full Bar
SERVING: Dinner
PRICE RANGE: $$
NEIGHBORHOOD: Edgefield
A no-frills bar that severs burgers. There's a deck, a dart board and a juke box.

EDLEY'S BAR-B-QUE
2706 12th Ave S, Nashville, 615-953-2951
www.edleybbq.com
CUISINE: Barbeque
DRINKS: Full Bar
SERVING: Lunch, Dinner
PRICE RANGE: $$
NEIGHBORHOOD: Belmont/Hillsboro
Lovers of BBQ flock to this Nashville institution for the food and hospitality. Menu favorites include: Pork Tacos and the Catfish sandwich. The meats are smoked fresh daily and they also serve homemade baked beans, mac and cheese, and cornbread.

EPICE
2902 12th Ave S, Nashville, 615-720-6765
www.epicenashville.com
CUISINE: Lebanese
DRINKS: Full Bar
SERVING: Lunch, Dinner
PRICE RANGE: $$
NEIGHBORHOOD: 12 South

Lovely eatery featuring nice selection of Lebanese fare. Menu favorites include: Tabouli, hummus, and the Eggplant and lamb with vermicelli rice. Imported wines.

ETCH
303 Demonbreun St, Nashville, 615-522-0685
www.etchrestaurant.com
CUISINE: New American
DRINKS: Full Bar
SERVING: Lunch weekdays (11-2 only); dinner nightly except Sunday, when it's closed
PRICE RANGE: $$$ to $$$$
NEIGHBORHOOD: Downtown
A classy, upscale restaurant serving food from what I consider to be one of the top 2 or 3 menus in Nashville. There's an open kitchen with seats at the bar so you can interact with the staff (if you care to). If you'd rather share an intimate meal with someone, go to one of the tables. Scallops on a bed of greens; octopus & shrimp bruschetta; rutabaga la plancha (simply wonderful); a grilled lamb T-bone; tempura okra; a sensational creation called the "Charcuterie Salad" consisting of Tennessee prosciutto, house cured sausages, yellow beet mustard puree, greens, spiced vinaigrette, smoked lima beans, pickled onion,

apple confit, fried oyster mushrooms—you've never had a salad like this before. The desserts are similarly creative: white chocolate lemon ganache.

F SCOTT'S RESTAURANT & JAZZ BAR
2400 West End Ave, Nashville, 615-269-5861; **(opening Fall 2014)**
www.fscotts.com
CUISINE: American
DRINKS: Full bar
SERVING: Dinner
PRICE RANGE: $$$
One of the nicest places in town, F. Scott's was relocating at press time to West End Avenue. Meantime, the same people are involved at a very nice brasserie called **Table 3.**

FIDO
1812 21st Ave S, Nashville, 615-777-3436
www.bongojava.com/fido-cafe
CUISINE: American; comfort
DRINKS: Beer & Wine
SERVING: Breakfast, Lunch, Dinner
PRICE RANGE: $$
NEIGHBORHOOD: Hillsboro/West End
This casual café offers a varied menu of organic, exotic and junk foods. Menu favorites include: the famous Local Burger (a mixture of beef & lamb) and the Liberal Salad. All desserts are made in-house. Breakfast is served all day.

FROTHY MONKEY
2509 12th Ave S, Nashville, 615-292-1808
www.frothymonkey.com
Has other locations in Nashville
CUISINE: American; coffeeshop; sandwich shop
DRINKS: Beer & Wine only
SERVING: Breakfast (from 7 am), Lunch & Dinner (till 9 pm)
PRICE RANGE: $

NEIGHBORHOOD: Belmont / Hillsboro / 12 South
Very reasonably priced place for a meal any time. Not only is it
cheap, but they're very serious about the sustainability of what
their serve here. They have gluten-free options, vegetarian &
vegan dishes, a special kids' menu, craft-inspired beer & wine
list. They support local vendors & suppliers. Look for the sign
out front with the monkey holding a coffee mug. Biscuits and
gravy with eggs; smoky asparagus & kale soup; French toast &
waffles; great selection of salads and hot and cold sandwiches.
For dinner, they have cider glazed pork with cinnamon sweet
potatoes; blackened shrimp & grits; a sausage burger and
blackened Gulf mahi. Also some great gift items from their
store: crocheted monkeys and other items.

GIOVANNI'S RISTORANTE
909 20th Ave S, Nashville, 615-760-5932
www.giovanninashville.com
CUISINE: Italian
DRINKS: Full Bar
SERVING: Lunch & Dinner
PRICE RANGE: $$$$
NEIGHBORHOOD: Midtown
You can get really sublime Italian cuisine here. Giovanni is one
of the stars of the burgeoning restaurant scene here in Nashville.
An elegant room with white tablecloths and fine crystal with
lovely arched windows looking outside. They have a traditional

menu that touches all the bases, but what's special here is how expertly everything is prepared.

GUS'S FRIED CHICKEN
471 Old Hickory Blvd, Brentwood, 615-331-4877
www.gusfriedchicken.com
CUISINE: American, Southern, Soul food
DRINKS: Beer & Wine
SERVING: Lunch, Dinner
PRICE RANGE: $
NEIGHBORHOOD: Brentwood
Chicken lovers fill this place for "Gus's World Famous Fried Chicken." Menu favorites: Crispy spicy fried chicken (of course). Everything else is secondary to the fried chicken. Very casual dining as food is served on Styrofoam picnic plates with plastic utensils.

HATTIE B'S
112 19th Ave S, Nashville, 615-678-4794

www.hattieb.com
CUISINE: American, Southern, Soul Food
DRINKS: Beer & Wine
SERVING: Lunch, Dinner
PRICE RANGE: $
NEIGHBORHOOD: Belmont/Vanderbilt
This place serves Nashville's "Hot Chicken" at its best. Menu favorites: Chick and Waffle special and Spicy chicken. Try the root beer float, a perfect combo with the chicken.

HERMITAGE CAFÉ
71 Hermitage Ave, Nashville, 615-254-8871
No Website
CUISINE: American, Diner
DRINKS: No Booze
SERVING: Breakfast, lunch, and late night. Closed for dinner.
PRICE RANGE: $
NEIGHBORHOOD: Downtown
Certainly not to be confused with the grand Hermitage Hotel, this old school diner serves your typical diner cuisine including "breakfast anytime." Menu favorites include: Veggie Omelet and Garden Burger, but I wouldn't eat those—gimme the sausages.

HOG HEAVEN BBQ

115 27th Ave N, Nashville, 615-329-1234

www.hogheavenbbq.com

CUISINE: Barbeque

DRINKS: No Booze

SERVING: Lunch, Early Dinner, Closed Sunday

PRICE RANGE: $

NEIGHBORHOOD: Belmont, Vanderbilt

Located next to Centennial Park, this place is famous for its "Kickin' Chicken" white BBQ sauce. One stop here will demonstrate why this place was featured on Food Network's "Best Thing I Ever Ate." Menu favorites include: Anything BBQ which includes pork, chicken, beef, and turkey. BBQ served in sandwiches, plates or by the pound. Outdoor seating or take-out.

HOLLAND HOUSE BAR AND REFUGE

935 W Eastland Ave, Nashville, 615-262-4190

www.hollandhousebarandrefuge.com

CUISINE: American

DRINKS: Beer & Wine only

SERVING: Dinner nightly except Sunday when it's closed

PRICE RANGE: $$

NEIGHBORHOOD: East Nashville

A large wooden door leads into this place where you'll find a red velvet Victorian loveseats, cut glass chandeliers hanging from the wood beamed ceiling casting a romantic light onto distressed brick walls. Outdoor seating in good weather. The menu is seasonal (as are the craft cocktails, which use seasonal ingredients). The chef brings classic French techniques to his work in the kitchen. Potted marrow with black garlic and preserved lemon; frisee & rabbit confit; cornmeal fried yellow tomatoes; tasso grilled catfish; roasted caprina goat; brined bone-in pork chop.

HONKY TONK CENTRAL

329 Broadway, Nashville, 615-742-9095

www.honkytonkcentral.com

CUISINE: American

DRINKS: Full Bar

SERVING: Lunch, Dinner & Late-night
PRICE RANGE: $$
NEIGHBORHOOD: Downtown
Very busy 3-story pub featuring live music. Menu is typical bar
grub like Tattor tots and deep-fried catfish. Huge bar and pub
menu. Large TV for sports fans.

HUSK
37 Rutledge St, Nashville, 615-256-6565
www.husknashville.com
CUISINE: New Southern
DRINKS: Full Bar
SERVING: Lunch & Dinner daily; weekend Brunch; indoor-
outdoor
PRICE RANGE: $$$
NEIGHBORHOOD: SoBro; Downtown
Just as he did when he made waves internationally in
Charleston, Chef Sean Brock has brought his song and dance act
to Nashville. As the chef puts it, "In Charleston it's all about the
sea; in Nashville, it's all about the dirt." Led by Brock, the
kitchen explores an ingredient-driven cuisine that begins in the
rediscovery of heirloom products and redefines what it means to
cook and eat in Nashville. The beautiful red brick building
where Husk is located was built into the side of a hill in the

1880s by Dr. John Bunyan Stephens. Its storied history includes serving as Mayor Richard Houston Dudley's home, where he lived when elected in 1897. The area was settled by the Rutledge and Middleton families of Charleston who were descendants of two of the original South Carolina signers of the Declaration of Independence. The design of the Husk's interior spaces enhances the building's roots while demonstrating a sense of Southern style, modernity, energy, and cosmopolitan flair. The classic red brick architecture is enhanced with super high and wide single-pane windows that look outside through the graceful arches on the porch and fill the dining room with light. Menu changes daily. Try the 24-month old country ham with mustard and pickled okra; fried chicken skins served with hot sauce & honey (bring your Lipitor); pimento cheese with Carolina rice cakes; short ribs and beets; shrimp & octopus grits; fried chicken that comes with mac & cheese & cabbage; fried chicken hearts & gizzards; a good bet here if you can visit it more than once is to get the vegetable plate—whatever they have, let them bring it out.

JOSEPHINE
2316 12 Ave S, Nashville, 615-292-7766
www.josephineon12th.com
CUISINE: American

DRINKS: Full Bar
SERVING: Dinner nightly from 5; Friday from 3; brunch on the weekends from 10
PRICE RANGE: $$$
NEIGHBORHOOD: Belmont / Hillsboro / 12 South
An elegant room with dark tufted banquettes against the far wall under a few very large mirrors. Maybe it's the lighting, but the crystal here just seems to "pop." I love the big square bar. Grilled chicken livers with pepper jelly; pickled shrimp; a great selection of fresh veggies; noodles and dumplings; pork jowl served with baby potatoes and pearl onions; grilled catfish; beef cheeks with a horseradish risotto. As tasty as everything else is, I invariably end up getting the Josephine steak frites with a round dollop of herb butter melting on top of the slices of meat. Dessert? Try the sorghum molasses tart with brown butter. Also the peach shortcake.

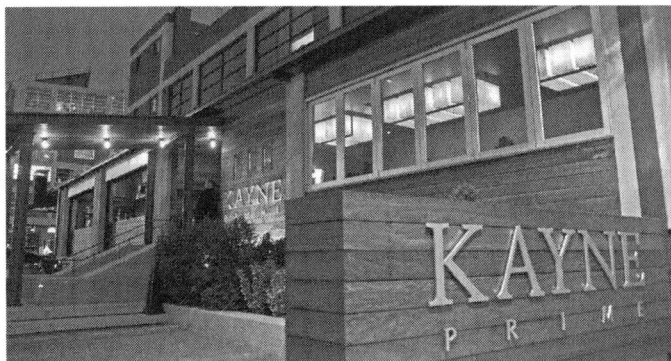

KAYNE PRIME
1304 McGavock St, Nashville, 615-259-0050
www.mstreetnashville.com/restaurants/kayne-prime
CUISINE: American
DRINKS: Full Bar
SERVING: Dinner nightly from 5
PRICE RANGE: $$$$
NEIGHBORHOOD: Downtown; Gulch
Handsome high-back banquettes against the wall. If you sit at the bar, you basically overlook a parking lot, but at night, when Downtown is ablaze with light, it's a different story entirely. 24-

ounce bone-in rib eye is spectacular (you can take what you don't eat home); a black kale salad that's much better than it sounds; whole fish of the day grilled or baked; house-made bacon (with a layer of fat on it that makes it look like a side of pork (I won't even discuss the bacon topped with cotton candy that they serve here—it's scary); broiled trout; mac gratinee that's beyond delicious; duck tacos.

KIEN GIANG
5845 Charlotte Pike, Nashville, 615-353-1250
No Website
CUISINE: Vietnamese
DRINKS: Beer & Wine Only
SERVING: Lunch & Dinner
PRICE RANGE: $ - cash only
Superior Vietnamese specialties in this nothing fancy hole-in-the-wall. The staff may seem brain dead, but I think they're just overworked. Whatever. Whoever is in the kitchen is not brain dead. Get the BBQ pork bahn mi, or the very popular Pho.

KRYSTAL
3715 Hillsboro Pike, Nashville, 615-292-8129
www.krystal.com
SERVING: Fast Food
DRINKS: No Booze
SERVING: Lunch, & Dinner
PRICE RANGE: $
NEIGHBORHOOD: Green Hills
This fast food eatery sells miniature hamburgers similar to the famous White Castle burgers. Certainly worth a "stop and eat."

THE LOCAL TACO
4501 Murphy Rd, Nashville, 615-891-3271
www.thelocaltaco.com
CUISINE: Mexican, Tex-Mex
DRINKS: Full Bar
SERVING: Lunch & Dinner
PRICE RANGE: $$
NEIGHBORHOOD: Sylvan Park
This is a taco eatery that's embraced the "locally sourced"
mantra. You won't get better tacos anywhere in town.

LOCKELAND TABLE
1520 Woodland St, Nashville, 615-228-4864
www.lockelandtable.com
CUISINE: American
DRINKS: Full Bar
SERVING: Dinner from 5 (bar opens at 4) except Sunday, when
it's closed
PRICE RANGE: $$$
NEIGHBORHOOD: East Nashville
Another one of those unassuming squat brick buildings you see
so often here in Nashville. Inside, however, there's a jumbled
design that makes you think they weren't sure what to settle on.

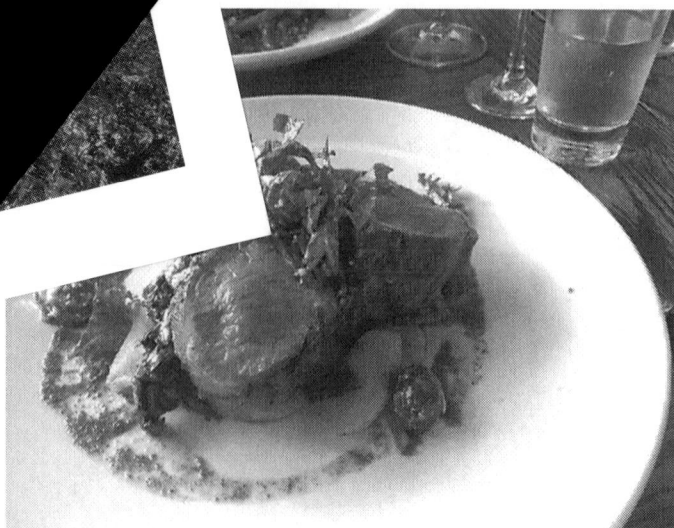

Lights hang from the ceiling amid the industrial look created by the a/c venting. Metal barstools lined up against the curved bar overlooking the kitchen. Somehow it all works beautifully. Smoked Cox Farms bone marrow; pork & shrimp dumplings; chicken liver paté in a jar; hot crispy pig ears; a modest selection of excellent pizzas; rack of lamb; Niman ranch bone-in pork loin; the freshwater trout is particularly good. (Make sure you get a side of the crab & corn fritters.)

THE LOVELESS CAFÉ
8400 Hwy 100, Nashville, 615-646-9700
www.lovelesscafe.com
CUISINE: American; Southern
DRINKS: Full Bar
SERVING: Breakfast, Lunch & Dinner
PRICE RANGE: $$
This is one of those places that's seared in the mind of everybody who grew up in Nashville. This is a "must" stop, even if it is a bit out of town. And yes, the waitresses will call

you, "Honey.") Try to go early or after peak hours because there's usually a waiting line, especially on weekends. And no, it's not just tourists. These are locals. A basket of biscuits comes with every order. It's as Southern as you can get. Everything's made from scratch. You can watch them pull their famous biscuits out of the oven because there's a window into the kitchen. Ham & eggs with red-eye gravy. Ever had a breakfast with pit-cooked BBQ pork and eggs? No? You can here. Steak biscuits (these are very popular) using grilled beef tenderloin; Southern sampler (country ham, bacon, sausage and eggs). If you come for dinner, you'll be just as pleased, however: fried pork chops; grilled catfish; country fried steak; fried chicken livers or gizzards (I used to love these gizzards as a child); homemade meatloaf. All the sides are just perfect, from the fried okra to the mac & cheese. They have an extensive shop and they've been shipping their goods out for decades (now on the Internet). Get gift packs with country ham & bacon; pantry goods; apparel and accessories; gifts; biscuits; preserves; items for the kitchen. Also be sure to check out the **Motel Shops** located in what used to be 14 rooms of the original motel that was behind the café. Stop by to grab some of their jams and preserves to take home.

MARCHÉ ARTISAN FOODS
1000 Main St, Nashville, 615-262-1111
www.marcheartisanfoods.com
CUISINE: Specialty Food
DRINKS: Beer & Wine
SERVING: Breakfast, Lunch & Dinner
PRICE RANGE: $$
NEIGHBORHOOD: East Nashville
Located in historic section of East Nashville, this European-style
café and marketplace offers a revolving menu. Menu favorites
include: Shrimp Grits and Pan Seared Pork Tenderloin and
Cornbread Panzanella. Breakfast served anytime. Great choice
for weekend brunch.

MARGOT CAFÉ & BAR
1017 Woodland St, Nashville, 615-227-4668
www.margotcafe.com
CUISINE: French, Italian
DRINKS: Full Bar
SERVING: Dinner
PRICE RANGE: $$$
NEIGHBORHOOD: Five Points; East Nashville
This is a special little intimate place, and many people in-the-know think this is perhaps "the" best restaurant owned by a chef in the whole of Nashville. (That's saying something.) Red brick walls with lots of mirrors hanging on them; wood tables for lunch; white tablecloths for dinner. Chef Margot earned her strips in the East Village before returning to Nashville to work at **F. Scott's** in Green hills. When she opened this place, she focused on the cuisines she loves most: southern France and parts of Italy, with an emphasis on the hearty, healthy peasant cuisines of these regions. The menu is seasonal and changes every day. Homemade potato chips; Minestra with broccoli pesto; pizza with veal, fava beans and ricotta; pan-roasted redfish; grilled pork chop with squash casserole. (To be honest, this is my first stop for dinner when I get to town.)

41

MAS TACOS POR FAVOR

732 McFerrin Ave, Nashville, 615-543-6271
www.eatmastacos.com
CUISINE: Mexican
DRINKS: No Booze
SERVING: Lunch, Dinner, Closed Sunday
PRICE RANGE: $
NEIGHBORHOOD: East Nashville
This popular "mobile eatery" (I love that term for a food truck)
offers a creative menu of tacos and soups. Menu favorites
include: Pulled Pork taco and Cast-iron chicken taco. Great
place for a fast weekend brunch.

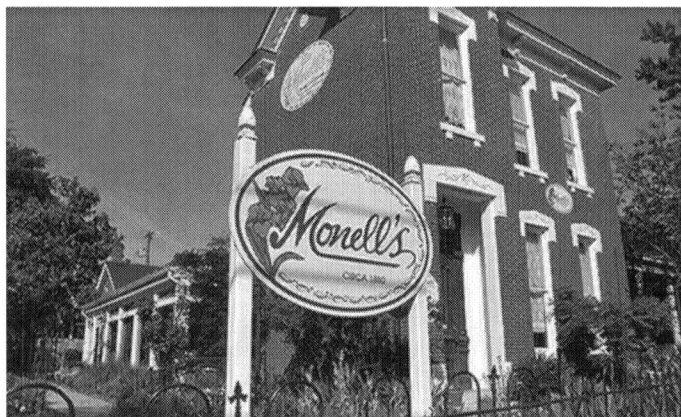

MONELL'S

1235 6th Ave N, Nashville, 615-298-2254
www.MonellsTn.com
CUISINE: Southern; soul food
DRINKS: No Booze
SERVING: Breakfast (from 10), Lunch & Dinner (till 7)
PRICE RANGE: $$
NEIGHBORHOOD: Germantown
I think the must use a shovel in the kitchen when they plate the
food, there's so much of it. Excellent Southern food served
family style. There's only a basic menu, with specials every day;
Monday, chicken & dumplings & meatloaf; Tuesday, spinach
lasagna and pot roast; Wednesday, pork chops, baked chicken

and fried chicken (they fry it in a skillet); and so on and so forth. Full country breakfast available. Excellent sides like fried apples, cheese grits, corn pudding. Whatever day it is, it will be good, I guarantee it.

THE PANCAKE PANTRY
1796 21st Ave S, Nashville, 615-383-9333
www.thepancakepantry.com
CUISINE: Bakeries, Breakfast
DRINKS: No Booze
SERVING: Breakfast & Lunch (6 a.m. to 3 p.m.)
PRICE RANGE: $$
NEIGHBORHOOD: Hillsboro, West End
You'll go crazy for the pancakes here—Swiss chocolate chip pancakes; especially the sweet potato pancakes served with a cinnamon syrup. There are over 20 varieties, like Santa Fe (cornmeal pancakes with bits of bacon, cheddar and green chilis), the Caribbean (buttermilk cakes with pecans, coconut, powdered sugar, slices of banana). It's hard to get a seat at one of the Formica tables here. The lines are very long, so plan on going early or late at off peak hours. There's plenty more on the menu if you're not eating carbs: sandwiches; burgers; ham and egg plates, lots more.

PEPPERFIRE HOT CHICKEN
2821 Gallatin Pike, Nashville, 615-582-4824
www.pepperfirechicken.com
CUISINE: Southern, Comfort Food
DRINKS: No Booze
SERVING: Lunch, Dinner; closed Sunday
PRICE RANGE: $
NEIGHBORHOOD: Gallatin Pike
This is a carry–out eatery only but there are picnic tables in front those too hungry to wait until they get home. The menu is a variety of chicken dishes and sandwiches—the deep-fried grilled cheese sandwich is well worth trying.

PHARMACY BURGER PARLOR AND BEER GARDEN
731 McFerrin, Nashville, 615-712-9527
www.thepharmacynashville.com
CUISINE: American; Burgers; pub fare
DRINKS: Beer & Wine
SERVING: Lunch & Dinner daily
PRICE RANGE: $$
NEIGHBORHOOD: East Nashville
Just a square white building from the outside, but inside there's a good vibe where locals meet to eat fantastic burgers and drink beer. Has an impressive selection of German wurst and German

beer. There's a Stroganoff Burger (mushroom stroganoff béchamel, sour cream, caramelized onion, Swiss cheese); among many others, as well as lots of German wursts: Jagerwurst, Bratwurst, Currywurst, Bauerwurst, Kielbasa, Bockwurst. Sides are handmade and uniformly excellent. Also there's an old-school sofa fountain serving up phosphates, milkshakes and ice cream sodas. In good weather, sit in the beer garden out back under the string of lights criss-crossing above you in the leafy canopy. (The ice cream here is particularly good.)

PRINCE'S HOT CHICKEN SHACK
123 Ewing Dr #3, Nashville, 615-226-9442
No Website
CUISINE: Southern
DRINKS: No Booze
SERVING: Lunch, Dinner; closed Sun & Mon
PRICE RANGE: $
NEIGHBORHOOD: Brooklyn Heights
Known as the pioneer of Hot Chicken, this place serves a variety of Hot Chicken in pieces, strips or whole. It's quite popular so expect a wait.
PUB5
104 5th Ave, Nashville, 615-780-4005
www.pub5.com

CUISINE: Pub fare; tapas
DRINKS: Full Bar
SERVING: Lunch & Dinner daily from 11
PRICE RANGE: $$
NEIGHBORHOOD: SoBro

Distressed brick walls, Edison lights hanging from the ceiling (I'm getting annoyed with these—they're showing up everywhere), a friendly bar scene, an outdoor patio area. Where you want to be is on the rooftop patio. Go for the pork belly tacos; a selection of meatballs (pork, beef, lamb, garlic polenta); charcuterie boards; crispy pork belly; lamb burger; smoke lamb ribs (I love these); fried chicken thighs (my favorite piece of the chicken) served with a potato hash cake. Desserts are OK, but the bread pudding is the standout.

PUCKETT'S GROCERY & REASTAURANT
500 Church St, Nashville, 615-770-2772
www.puckettsgrocery.com
CUISINE: American
DRINKS: Full Bar
SERVING: Breakfast, Lunch, Dinner daily
PRICE RANGE: $$
NEIGHBORHOOD: Downtown

Great location in a corner building in Downtown. Not only is it a good restaurant, but there's a store and live music as well on the little stage on one side of the dining room. Ultra casual atmosphere. Your drinks come in mason jars. Pulled pork sliders; fried pickles & jalapenos; fried green tomatoes & chipotle dip; cherry-smoked hot wings; Southern fried catfish; Piggy Mac (smoked pulled pork in an iron skillet topped with smoked gouda mac & cheese); smoked baby back ribs. (Get the Maple Pecan Pie if you can manage it after stuffing yourself with all this comfort food.) If you're here for breakfast, try the Bubba's Eggs Benedict (split biscuits topped with bacon or sausage covered with 2 fried eggs and smothered in pepper gravy).

ROLF AND DAUGHTERS
700 Taylor St, Nashville, 615-866-9897
www.rolfanddaughters.com
CUISINE: American, Mediterranean
DRINKS: Full Bar
SERVING: Dinner
PRICE RANGE: $$$

NEIGHBORHOOD: Germantown
This restaurant, run by Chef Philip Krajeck, offers a beautiful dining experience in a refurbished Werthan packaging factory that's a century old. It has brick walls, old slats of reclaimed wood on the high ceiling above and these tall wide windows with no drapes or anything that gives it a workhouse look. At the long dorm style common table stretching down the center, you almost expect to see Oliver Twist eating his gruel. A great atmosphere. The Belgian-raised Chef Krajeck is famous around these parts not for his gruel, but for his fresh pasta. Among the more unique eateries in town, Rolf combines Southern food with a Northern Italian - Mediterranean twist. Menu favorites include: Crispy-Skinned Chicken; Pork Tenderloin; chicken-liver pate served with a green tomato jam; meatballs and dandelion greens.

SAFFIRE
230 Franklin Rd, Franklin, 615-599-4995
http://saffirerestaurant.com
CUISINE: American
DRINKS: Full Bar
SERVING: Lunch Tuesday-Sunday 11-3; Dinner Tuesday-Sunday from 5; closed Monday

PRICE RANGE: $$$
An upmarket spot that's fun and unpretentious, in an industrial
style atmosphere. It's about 15 minutes out of town on I-65
South. It's located in the "Factory at Franklin" shopping center,
and is well worth the drive for its excellent cuisine. Much of
their food is supplied by local vendors (Bear Creek Farm,
Charpiers Bakery, Jones Mill Farm, Delvin Farms), and they're
serious about their work. Corn meal fried avocado; lobster
empanadas; steak biscuits (with blue cheese and horseradish);
Creole shrimp & grits; a lovely peach glazed pork chop.
Occasionally, they have live music.

SILO
1121 5th Ave N, Nashville, 615-750-2912
www.silotn.com
CUISINE: Southern; bistro
DRINKS: Full Bar
SERVING: Dinner daily at 5; bar opens at 4 for happy hour;
Sunday brunch from 10:30
PRICE RANGE: $$
NEIGHBORHOOD: Germantown
A simple red brick building with floor-to-ceiling windows
looking outside. Inside, it's wood, wood, wood, from the tables
to the chairs to the walls. The tables were made by a local artisan
from Ethridge, Tennessee. The pendant lights came from another
artist in Louisville. The space features a community table, a
private dining room, a large bar area, two patios and an open
kitchen. One of the owners came from the French Culinary
Institute and the other one from a bakery in Charleston, so you
have a heady mix of Southern food with French bistro twists.
Smokey pork spare ribs with a Coco Cola BBQ sauce; baby
beets and sautéed kale; cast iron scallion-jalapeno cornbread;
chicken confit; hangar steak. If you come for Sunday Brunch,
get the pulled pork eggs Benedict style with a jalapeno
hollandaise to create a nice bite that'll wake you right up.

SLOCO

2905 12th Ave S, Nashville, 615-499-4793

www.slocolocal.com
CUISINE: Sandwiches
DRINKS: No booze
SERVING: 9 am to 5 pm
PRICE RANGE: $
NEIGHBORHOOD: Belmont / Hillsboro / 12 South

Here they promise sustainably sourced food at affordable prices, and they mean it. And if the food is not in season, they don't have it and don't truck it in. Sandwiches like Ham & Cheese (Sorghum cured ham); Cordon bleu; Pesto chicken; my favorite, the Redneck Reuben (caraway slaw, Swiss-style cheese, Dijon, corned pork shoulder). Lots of others. Wash it down with a Blue Sky Root Beer. Each sandwich has a "Miles Traveled" notation which tells you how far each of the ingredients in your particular sandwich traveled to get to their kitchen. (I wish they'd require this in EVERY restaurant so we could all see where in the world some of the food we eat comes from—it would change how we ordered our meals, I guarantee it. The only lies greater than the ones coming out of Washington are to be found on restaurant menus.)

SOUTHERN STEAK & OYSTER
150 3rd Ave S, Nashville, 615-724-1762
www.thesouthernnashville.com
CUISINE: American; New Southern
DRINKS: Full Bar
SERVING: Breakfast weekdays from 7:30; Lunch daily; Dinner nightly (but bar opens for happy hour at 3); brunch on weekends from 10 am
PRICE RANGE: $$$
NEIGHBORHOOD: Downtown; SoBro
Has a very New York feel with its subway style bathroom white-tiled floor, expansive back bar and thin-strips of wood in the ceiling. This is a very good place for breakfast: Southern omelet (braised pork, onions, collards, black-eyes peas, cheddar, served with grits or potatoes); smoked brisket with jalapeno cheddar

grits and 2 fried eggs; or the fried egg sandwich. Later on, I like the daily selection of oysters. They usually have two or 3 types. Also the Dominican braised pork; bahn mi tacos; double-cut smoked pork chop; baby back ribs; dry aged strip steak.

SUNSET GRILL
2001 Belcourt Ave, Nashville, 615-386-3663
www.sunsetgrill.com
CUISINE: American
DRINKS: Full Bar
SERVING: Dinner
PRICE RANGE: $$
NEIGHBORHOOD: 21st & Vanderbilt, Hillsboro, West End
Consistently voted one of Nashville's best restaurants, this friendly place in Hillsboro Village has an excellent, inexpensive late-night menu. Focuses on Italian and Mediterranean cuisine, and has a large selection of fine wines. Good dessert and wine list.

TABLE 3
3821 Green Hills Village Dr, Nashville, 615-739-6900
www.table3nashville.com
CUISINE: American; French brasserie-bistro
DRINKS: Full Bar

SERVING: Lunch and dinner daily; Sunday brunch menu
PRICE RANGE: $$
NEIGHBORHOOD: Green Hills
With dark wood accents and lots of glass, this is a welcoming place where you can get very good French specialties (my favorite is the cassoulet, as it's so hard to find and they do quite a serviceable job here); French onion soup; crispy duck confit; beef short ribs bourguignon; duck burger' croquet madame. There's also a Market & Bakery here that opens at 9 a.m.

TAVERN
1904 Broadway, Nashville, 615-320-8580
http://mstreetnashville.com/restaurants/tavern
CUISINE: Gastro pub; some Asian; some Mexican
DRINKS: Full Bar
SERVING: Lunch and Dinner daily; Brunch on weekends from 10 am; open till 3 am Friday & Saturday
PRICE RANGE: $$ to $$$

NEIGHBORHOOD: Downtown

Wraparound booths create a cozy atmosphere within the lively bar scene in this high-ceilinged room. A half-raised mezzanine level lets you look down on the bar scene while you eat. Later in the evening, they shift to more energetic beat, with DJs cranking out the tunes. (They stay open till about 3 am on Friday and Saturday.) Lots of TVs for the sports-inclined. Has one of the better brunches on weekends. Small plates like wood-grilled artichokes; egg rolls; fried chicken skins; chili scallops. A great selection of creative tacos: fish, lamb, chicken, short ribs. Also an impressive line-up of salads and sandwiches; mahi, tuna salad, lobster sliders, patak bratwurst, as well as a great burger. Main plates include grilled hamburger steak with a fried egg on top; a basket of crispy little fish (cornmeal fried catfish); lots of specialty cocktails. If you're here for brunch, get the White Trash Hash and the Benedict Uno with braised short ribs. The brunches are very busy.

TWO TEN JACK

1900 Eastland Ave #105, Nashville, 615-454-2731
www.twotenjack.com
CUISINE: Ramen
DRINKS: Full Bar
SERVING: Dinner, closed Sun
PRICE RANGE: $$
NEIGHBORHOOD: Lockeland Springs

A Japanese-inspired neighborhood pub that offers a menu of kodawari ramen, skewers & grilled items, sushi and Japanese inspired pub comfort food. Handcrafted cocktails.

VIRAGO

1126 McGavock St, Nashville, 615-254-1902
http://mstreetnashville.com/restaurants/virago
CUISINE: Japanese; robata grill & sushi bar
DRINKS: Full Bar
SERVING: Dinner nightly from 5
PRICE RANGE: $$$
NEIGHBORHOOD: Downtown; Gulch

Has a strikingly modern design inside with a slanted ceiling held up by stark metal posts; wood and brick, recessed lighting.

Lobster tacos; crispy Brussels sprouts; Tsukune chicken meatballs; bacon wrapped scallops; Mune chicken breast; smoked brisket Udon; tuffled black grouper; salt & pepper shrimp. There's a very nice rooftop bar with a view of Downtown, so go up there if you can.

WHISKEY KITCHEN
118 12th Ave S, Nashville, 615-254-3029
www.mstreetnashville.com
CUISINE: American (New)
DRINKS: Full Bar
SERVING: Lunch, Dinner
PRICE RANGE: $$
NEIGHBORHOOD: Downtown
Popular bar with a menu of tavern grub. Menu favorites include: Blackbean burger, Braised beef short ribs and Whiskey brownie cheesecake.

Chapter 4
NIGHTLIFE

THE 5 SPOT
1006 Forrest Ave., Nashville, 615-650-9333
http://the5spotlive.com/blog/
NEIGHBORHOOD: East Nashville, near Five Points
This long narrow bar with a stage at the far end is a great spot
for dancing, cheap beer, lots of live music, offering up multiple
acts every night except Monday. There's a modest menu
offering a couple of pizzas and some sandwiches if you want a
snack. They have a gay dance party on the third Friday of every
month called **QDP (Queer Dance Party).**

THE BASEMENT
1604 8th Ave S, Nashville, 615-254-8006
www.thebasementnashville.com

This small venue books a wide variety of music acts, from country singer to indie bands. Check the web site for schedule. No smoking inside. 21 and over. If you go upstairs, you'll find one of the best indie record stores in town (maybe even the country), **Grimey's New & Preloved Music.**

BLUEBIRD CAFÉ
4104 Hillsboro Pike, Nashville, 615-383-1461
www.bluebirdcafe.com
If you're a singer or a songwriter, performing here is like a "coming of age" experience. They usually have 2 shows a night. The cozy (OK, tight and crowded) room that seats only 100 lucky customers is actually a good thing, not a bad thing. You feel like you're seeing tomorrow's stars, and in many cases, you really are. If you're a fan of the show "Nashville," you've seen what you think is this place on TV. Though they perform on a set (accurate even down to the line of lights strung along the bar), it's uncanny how well they captured this place. The walls are plastered with pictures of some of the thousands of musicians who've performed here. You'll want to reserve a seat, but reservations open usually Monday at 8 a.m. for the shows that week. They go fast. They serve food, but it's not that good, so eat elsewhere and come here for the show. Plan on showing up early. They will give your reserved seat to someone else if you're a minute late.

BOBBY'S IDLE HOUR

1028 16th Ave S, Nashville, 615-726-0446
www.bobbysidlehour.com
A dive bar with live music. Wednesday and Thursday night
jams. A favorite hangout of local songwriters. People on the way
up in the music business gather here, as well as people on the
way down.

BONGO JAVA

2007 Belmont Blvd, Nashville, 615-385-5282
www.bongojava.com
NEIGHBORHOOD: Belmont, Hillsboro
Right across the street from Belmont University is this place
that's a hangout for lots of artists, students, musicians and those
who want to be around them. You can mix and mingle with
them over a cup of coffee or a snack. Try the Juanita Burrita (3
eggs, grilled onions & jalapenos with chipotle cream cheese &
jack cheese in a tortilla—comes with hashbrowns and house
salsa). They also have burgers, several sandwiches, tacos, grilled
cheese, salads. Above the coffeeshop is the **Bongo After Hours
Theatre**, which showcases theatre, musical events, improve,
classes and workshops.

CRYING WOLF

823 Woodland St, Nashville, 615-953-6715
www.thecryingwolf.com
A no-frills bar that also serves burgers.

EAST NASHVILLE

Across the Cumberland River is the hippest area of town called
East Nashville. This is where the more cutting edge segment of
the population lives and works and hangs out (the artists, the
musicians, etc.), and you'd be doing yourself a disservice if you
don't venture over here. It's East Nashville that's giving the
town its international press, not Downtown. Just as in any other
town where these people congregate, the restaurants,
coffeehouses, cafes, nightclubs, lounges and shops have
sprouted up to serve their needs.

DOUGLAS CORNER CAFÉ

2106A 8th Ave S, Nashville, 615-298-1688
www.douglascorner.com
NEIGHBORHOOD: 12 South
You can experience real country music here, whether it's a local
act or a touring group. Every month (on the last Wednesday), a
group called **45rpm** offers up traditional country music. Not to
be missed.

THE END

2219 Elliston Pl, Nashville, 615-321-4457
www.endnashville.com
This is another great venue where you can hear excellent indie
rock bands, both local and national.

GRAND OLE OPRY HOUSE

2804 Opryland Drive, Nashville, 615-871-6604
www.opry.com
The live-performance radio program that put Nashville on the
map is still going strong, even after the horrendous 2010 flood
that wrecked the building. All is well, however, in the
refurbished venue. Even if you HATE country music, you've got
to make an effort to squeeze this into your itinerary. There's a
backstage tour of the facility. You'll be able to stand onstage
where thousands of legendary performers have stood "in the
circle." You'll learn the history of the Opry (it started at the
Ryman Auditorium downtown) and how it developed, and all of

it is very interesting. You'll get to see the old studio where "Hee Haw" was filmed, and you'll get to see a show running a couple of hours featuring a steady stream of entertainers, comedians, singers. This will likely be the standout experience of your visit if you make the plunge and do it. It's something you'll never forget as long as you live.

THE HIGH WATT
1 Cannery Row, Nashville, 615-251-3020
www.thehighwatt.com
A cozy little club housed in a century-old former cannery showcases local up and coming bands and national talents. 500 capacity music venue with a back bar that features pool tables and booth seating.

HONKEY TONK CENTRAL
329 Broadway, Nashville, 615-742-9095
www.honkytonkcentral.com
Very busy 3-story pub featuring live music. Huge bar and pub menu. Large TV for sports fans. It's a big-time tourist trap.

HURRY BACK
2212 Elliston Pl, Nashville, 615-915-0764
www.hurry-back.com
Great selection of rare and craft beers. Bar fare menu. TVs and big projector for sports. Outdoor seating.

MELROSE BILLIARDS
2600 Franklin Pike, Nashville, 615-383-9201
No Website
This is a true dive bar filled with lots of old-time regulars. Cheap prices, pool tables, ping pong, and snooker. Everybody from construction workers to studio musicians.

NO. 308
407 Gallatin Ave, Nashville, 615-650-7344
www.bar308.com/
Trendy late-night hangout serving craft cocktails. Patio seating and popular happy hour. (Get the 308 sliders if you're hungry.)

OAK BAR
THE HERMITAGE HOTEL
231 Sixth Ave N, Nashville, 615-345-7116
http://www.capitolgrillenashville.com/oak-bar
NEIGHBORHOOD: Downtown; Lower Broadway
Though I'm putting this in the nightlife chapter, it's also a
perfect place to meet for a drink before dinner, or to come when
winding down the evening for a Cognac after dinner or a show.
Opens at 11:30 for drinks and also has a casual menu (fried
pickles; smoked bologna sandwich; Granny's deviled eggs;
hunter's plate of house-cured smoked meats and pickled items;
Brunswick stew; BBQ shrimp; the Tennessee Stack is two 4-
ounce Double H beef patties with cheddar, pepper jelly, sweet
onion and hot mustard), and is open for happy hour from 4:30 to
6:30.

PARADISE PARK TRAILER RESORT
411 Broadway, Nashville, 615-251-1515
www.paradiseparkonline.com/
Popular trailer-park-themed eatery serving diner fare.
Live music. Open 24/7. Cheap pitchers of beer. 24
types of beer on tap. It's really the kind of place
people who work in offices come to pretend they're
white trash.

PINEWOOD SOCIAL
33 Peabody St, Nashville, 615-751-8111
www.pinewoodsocial.com
Trendy industrial-chic hangout open all day. The location used
to be a trolley car depot, so it has a funky charm. The place is
divided into three parts—couches in the front section are nice for
a cup of Crema coffee in the morning; the middle section is great
for innovative cocktails and some food (the catfish sandwich is
my favorite); the section in the back is where they have vintage
bowling lanes and karaoke. In the summer, there's even a pool
on the patio.

THE PATTERSON HOUSE
1711 Division St, Nashville, 615-636-7724
www.thepattersonnashville.com
This dark, luxurious bar throwing off a speakeasy vibe and
sporting vintage chandeliers and rows of bookshelves serves
delicious old-fashioned cocktails late into the night. There's a
velvet curtain you pass through, a bar in the center with stools
and a series of booths against the walls lit by candles. They are
very serious about the craft cocktails served here, down to the
point that they make their own bitters in house. Bacon Old
Fashioned has maple syrup in it; the classic Sidecar is served,
one of my favorite drinks. The small plate menu items are all
made to order, from the potato chips to the truffled deviled eggs;
beef sliders & tater tots; cinnamon sugar donuts; fig & prosciutto
flatbread (and don't overlook the donut holes). One of my all-
time favorite places in Nashville.

ROBERT'S WESTERN WORLD
416B Broadway, Nashville, 615-244-9552
www.robertswesternworld.com
NEIGHBORHOOD: Downtown
In Nashville, when you say you're going "honky-tonking," it
means you're going out on the town. This is one of the best
places to do that. A super variety of great musical acts fills their
schedule. You can't miss their big sign right on Broadway with
the lit up guitar. Also has good white trash food: fried Bolonga
sandwiches, grilled cheese, cheap burgers that are so juicy and
flavorful, really good hot dogs. I don't know anybody who
doesn't absolutely love this place. When it's really crowded on
Friday and Saturday nights, go to the back-alley entrance next to
the Ryman Auditorium where you'll find a doorman who's
checking IDs, but you can still get in with less hassle.

SANTA'S PUB
2225 Bransford Ave, Nashville, 615-593-1872
www.santaspub.com
Busy dive bar located in a triple-wide trailer. Holiday décor all
year with cheap beer and karaoke that seems to be continuous.

You can miss the mural of the Santa on the motorcycle on the front of the building. Cash only.

SPRINGWATER
115 27th Ave N, Nashville, 615-320-0345
www.springwatersupperclub.com
My younger readers won't know who he is, but Jimmy Hoffa used to hang out here in one of the best beer-only dive bars in Nashville that once-upon-a-time was a speakeasy. It's located next to Centennial Park. You'll encounter a bunch of drunks spending their Social Security checks, college kids looking to slum it. But the jukebox is good and they have arcade games.

THE STAGE ON BROADWAY
412 Broadway, Nashville, 615-726-0504
www.thestageonbroadway.com
A Honky-Tonk that mixes the flavor of Texas with Nashville. Live country music and a dance floor. Never a cover charge. Country music for people wearing flip flops.

STATION INN
402 12th Ave S, Nashville, 615-255-3307
www.stationinn.com

NEIGHBORHOOD: Downtown; Gulch

When you first get a glimpse of this plain concrete building, you get the sense that this place doesn't really belong here because the Gulch area has become so trendy, with expensive new condos rising around it. But this is one of the top destinations in town because of its excellent bluegrass and old-time shows that continue to attract crowds, as they have for many years. Every time I go there, I hear brilliant music, especially bluegrass and Western swing. On any given night, while you down your Bud Light and eat popcorn, you might see Ronnie Bowman, Guy Clark or another, younger player everyone's going to be talking about in a couple years.

STONE FOX
712 51st Ave N, Nashville, 615-953-1811
www.thestonefoxnashville.com
Rustic restaurant with a bar vibe offering American food & weekend brunch. Live music.

THE SUTLER SALOON
2600 Franklin Pike, Nashville, 615-840-6124
www.thesutler.com

Rustic-chic late-night hangout serving craft cocktails and Southern fare. Live music.

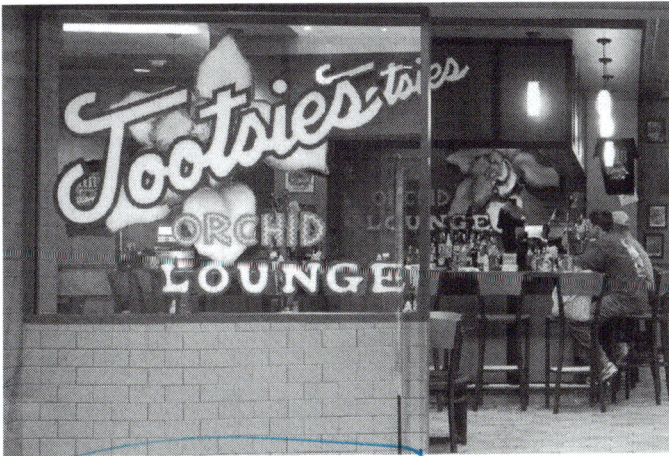

TOOTSIE'S ORCHID LOUNGE
422 Broadway, Nashville, 615-726-0463
www.tootsies.net/
One of Nashville's original Honky Tonks. The place is filled with memories and photos of bands that have played there. Great place to hang out and watch the locals mingle with the musicians who fill the place. Willie Nelson grew up signing here and Patsy Cline used to drink here. Kristofferson used to hang out here as well.

WHISKEY KITCHEN
118 12th Ave S, Nashville, 615-254-3029
www.mstreetnashville.com
Busy and welcoming watering hole featuring a menu of global whiskeys and tavern fare. This is a good place to begin your tour of the area's nightlife opportunities.

Chapter 5
WHAT TO SEE & DO

ADVENTURE SCIENCE CENTER
800 Fort Negley Blvd, Nashville, 615-862-5160
www.adventuresci.org
This institution seeks to inspire curiosity in all things scientific, and to encourage a lifelong discovery of science. They've been here since 1945. With 44,000 square feet of exhibit space, the Center features nearly 200 hands-on exhibits focused on biology, physics, visual perception, listening, mind, air and space, energy and earth science. A great place to bring the kids,

though I go all by myself. Their award-winning programs include daily science demonstrations, Discovery Cart activities, workshops, lectures, camps, Science Cafes and other special events. The **Sudekum Planetarium** features state-of-the-art digital projection and surround sound to present programs on a wide range of sciences, history, culture and laser shows.

BELLE MEADE PLANTATION
110 Leake Ave, Nashville, 615-356-0501
www.bellemeadeplantation.com
There's an ancient log cabin on the grounds of this beautiful old plantation that dates back to 1790, but more interesting is the plantation itself that dates back to 1853 (the carriage house was added in 1890). Guided tours are filled with interesting historical information. Modest fee.

BELMONT MANSION
1700 Acklen Ave, Nashville, 615-460-5459
www.belmontmansion.com
NEIGHBORHOOD: Belmont, Hillsboro
This is one of the top attractions in town, and is the biggest "house museum" in Tennessee. The moving spirit behind Belmont Mansion is Adelicia Hayes Franklin Acklen Cheatham.

She was born on 1817,into a prominent Nashville family. At the age of 22, Adelicia married her first husband, Isaac Franklin, a wealthy businessman and plantation owner who was 28 years her senior. They had four children, all of whom died before the age of 11. After seven years of marriage, Isaac Franklin died unexpectedly of a stomach virus while visiting one of his plantations in Louisiana. Adelicia inherited a huge estate including: 8,700 acres of cotton plantations in Louisiana; Fairvue, a 2,000-acre farm in Tennessee; more than 50,000 acres of undeveloped land in Texas; stocks and bonds; and 750 slaves. In 1846, at the age of 29, Adelicia Franklin was independently wealthy, worth about $1 million. In 1849, she remarried, to Joseph Alexander Smith Acklen, a Mexican War hero and a lawyer from Huntsville, Alabama. Together they built Belmont Mansion (originally named Belle Monte), completing construction in 1853. You'll definitely want to take the guided tour of the 16 rooms on the tour.

BICENTENNIAL CAPITOL MALL STATE PARK
600 James Robertson Pkwy, Nashville, 615-741-5280
http://tnstateparks.com/parks/about/bicentennial-mall
NEIGHBORHOOD: Downtown

In this park laid out before the Capitol you'll see a huge 200-foot large granite map of Tennessee, but it offers other features that make it the No. 1 attraction in all of Nashville: the farmers' market, the fish market, a nursery, fountains where you'll see kids playing, a large WW II memorial, a 95-bell Carillon, the Pathway of History and the Rivers of Tennessee Fountains. The 11 planters along the Walkway of Counties show native plant species from different regions of the state. The two-page park map is a helpful and informative tool for those wishing to take a self-guided tour of the park. Park rangers provide interpretive park tours, historical presentations in period dress and off-site programs by reservation. Program topics illustrate Tennessee's rich history from early settlement days to present time. To schedule an interpretive tour, presentation or off-site program, you can call 615-741-5771.

CARNTON PLANTATION
1345 Eastern Flank Circle, Nashville, 615-794-0903
www.carnton.org

On the site of this plantation there was a big Civil War confrontation between the Unikon and confederate armies known as the Battle of Franklin. You can take a comprehensive walking tour of this battlefield. Tour guides focus on many elements of the Battle of Franklin, explaining why it occurred, the arrival of the Federal and Confederate armies, and the details of what became known as one of the greatest single assaults of the Civil War. (There is a fee.) Battlefield Tours are offered Tuesday through Friday at 11 A.M. Reservations are encouraged, but not required. Carnton was built in 1826 by former Nashville mayor Randal McGavock (1768-1843). Throughout the nineteenth century it was frequently visited by those shaping Tennessee and American history, including President Andrew Jackson. Carnton grew to become one of the premier farms in Williamson County. Beginning at 4 p.m. on November 30, 1864, Carnton was witness to one of the bloodiest battles of the entire Civil War. Everything the McGavock family ever knew was forever changed. The Confederate Army of Tennessee furiously assaulted the Federal army entrenched along the southern edge of Franklin. The resulting battle, believed to be the bloodiest five hours of the Civil War, involved a massive frontal assault larger than Pickett's Charge at Gettysburg. The majority of the combat occurred in the dark and at close quarters. The Battle of Franklin lasted barely five hours and led to some 9,500 soldiers being killed, wounded, captured, or counted as missing. Nearly 7,000 of that number were Confederate troops. Carnton served as the largest field hospital in the area for hundreds of wounded and dying Confederate soldiers. A staff officer later wrote that "the wounded, in hundreds, were brought to [the house] during the battle, and all the night after. And when the noble old house could hold no more, the yard was appropriated until the wounded and dead filled that...." On the morning of December 1, 1864 the bodies of four Confederate generals killed during the fighting, Patrick R. Cleburne, Hiram B. Granbury, John Adams, and Otho F. Strahl, lay on Carnton's back porch. The floors of the restored home are still stained with the blood of the men who were treated here, and you can see these stains.

COUNTRY MUSIC HALL OF FAME & MUSEUM
222 5th Ave S, Nashville, 615-416-2001
www.countrymusichalloffame.org
NEIGHBORHOOD: Downtown
They have doubled the original size of this museum and added
lots more exhibits. The tours here are all self-guided.
WSM radio personality Bill Cody takes you on a tour through
the different eras of country music and his narrative provides
behind the scenes stories, insider tips, personal memories and
more. With the newly expanded exhibit space, they suggest
allowing approximately 2-3 hours to experience the museum.
However, depending upon your own pace or if you decide to
participate in any of their programs, you may like to stay longer.
 Your ticket is good all day, so you may come and go as needed.
There's so much for you to explore. You can see Bill Monroe's
mandolin, Elvis Presley's shiny Cadillac, tacky as all get-out
with its ground-up pearls, diamonds and fish scales. Oh, and
hundreds of guitars. Aside from the Museum and Hall of Fame,
they also offer tours of **Historic RCA Studio B** (Nashville's
only historic studio tour) and **Hatch Show Print** (one of
America's oldest letterpress print shops). Allow approximately
an hour for each tour. Shop in one of four retail stores and have
lunch or a snack in their full-service restaurant, **Two Twenty-
Two Grill.**

74

FAIRGROUNDS SPEEDWAY
625 Smith Ave, Nashville, 615-254-1986
www.fairgroundsspeedwaynashville.com/
Located on the Tennessee State Fairgrounds, this is the second
oldest continually operating track in the United States.

FRIST CENTER FOR THE VISUAL ARTS
919 Broadway, Nashville, 615-244-3340
www.fristcenter.org
NEIGHBORHOOD: Downtown
The Frist Center opened in April 2001 (in a gorgeous Art Deco
building that once housed the post office), and since that time
has hosted a spectacular array of art from the region, the
country, and around the world. It's become a magnet for
Nashville's rapidly expanding visual arts scene. With an
exhibitions schedule that has new art flowing through the
magnificent Art Deco building every 6 to 8 weeks, no matter
how often you visit, there is always something new and exciting
to see in the spacious galleries. The Frist Center was conceived
as a family-friendly place and one of the most popular locations
in the center is the innovative **Martin ArtQuest Gallery**. With
30 interactive stations, and the assistance of knowledgeable staff
and volunteers, ArtQuest teaches through activity. Make a print,
paint your own original watercolor, create your own colorful
sculpture. It's all there in ArtQuest, and it's free with gallery

admission for adults and always free for youth 18 and under. While at the Frist Center, be sure to stop by the **Gift Shop**. There, you'll find a fabulous array of art prints, books, educational materials, art supplies, clothing, blown glass, pottery, and magnificent jewelry made by local and regional artisans. Items are available in a wide range of prices, so there's always something to fit your budget. Because much of the merchandise relates to the Frist Center's exhibitions, the selection changes often. (It might even be the best gift shop in Nashville. The popular Frist Center **Café** features a variety of homemade soups, desserts, salads, and sandwiches, making the Café a popular gathering place for brunch, lunch, afternoon snacks, and dinner on Thursday and Friday evenings when the Frist Center stays open until 9 p.m.

GENERAL JACKSON SHOWBOAT
2812 Opryland Drive, Nashville, 615-458-3900
www.generaljackson.com
This 300-foot-long paddlewheel boat offers Midday Cruises, Sunday Brunch and Evening Cruises, including buffet and show. It's the only thing like it in Nashville. After the meal on the Midday Cruise, you get a country music variety show, **Nashville Live**. The world-class cast includes two rising country artists, an

internationally acclaimed trick-roper, a country comedian and features fiddle and guitar soloists, all supported by a live country band. The show's repertoire spans classic hits by Patsy Cline, George Jones and Tammy Wynette through today's chart-topping hits by Jason Aldean, Taylor Swift and Rascal Flatts. The Evening Cruise offers the same great views of downtown Nashville and followed by the show, from bluegrass to soul, a little gospel and, of course, country music. Covering classic Elvis to the new artists of country music, the cast of seven is backed by a live six-piece band. The Sunday Brunch Cruise you get a Southern buffet, and afterwards, a vocal quartet and three instrumentalists singing "Down by the Riverside," "Good Ole Gospel Ship," "Get All Excited" and other traditional Southern Gospel favorites and contemporary Christian music with songs like "Your Grace is Enough" and "I Could Sing of Your Love Forever."

HELISTAR AVIATION
110 Tune Airport Drive, Nashville, 615-350-1122
www.flyhelistar.com
Helicopter tours.

THE HERMITAGE
4580 Rachels Lane, Nashville, 615-889-2941
www.thehermitage.com
Constructed from 1819 to 1821 by skilled carpenters and masons
from the local area, the original section of the Hermitage
mansion was a brick Federal-style house. This design was a
typical plantation dwelling for aspiring gentleman farmers in the
Upper South but was already beginning to lose favor in more
fashionable Eastern areas. The house contained eight rooms—
four on each floor—and two wide center halls. This symmetrical
center hall style plan held its popularity in the South for many
years, and in fact was used in my Godparents' house, Marston
Plantation, in Stateburg, S.C., so when I first walked in here, I
felt right at home. The first floor contained two parlors, a dining
room, and Andrew and Rachel Jackson's bedroom. The upstairs
held four bedrooms. The elegant house featured a basement
summer kitchen, nine fireplaces, an entrance fanlight, French
wallpaper, and metal gutters. Later, Jackson added a small plain
entrance portico.

In 1831, while Jackson was President, he undertook a major remodeling directed by architect David Morrison. Morrison dramatically renovated the mansion with flanking one-story wings, a two-story entrance portico with ten Doric columns, a small rear portico, and copper gutters. The east wing contained a library and farm office while a large dining room and pantry comprised the west wing. A new kitchen and smokehouse were also built behind the 13-room mansion. Morrison's remodeling gave the house a new Classical appearance. Lots of Jackson's possessions are on display. The mansion is surrounded by extensive grounds. There's a great gift shop here, too.

HONKY TONK HIGHWAY

Bars and clubs are called "honky tonks" here in Nashville. Broadway in Downtown is where you want to be. There's a never-ending series of bars that provide a wide range of live music. You'll encounter even more musicians out on the sidewalks earning their keep from tips from people like you passing by. Neon signs line the whole street, giving the place an other-worldly glow. The TV show "Nashville" has filmed inside some of the bars, including **Layla's Bluegrass Inn** and

Tootsie's Orchid Lounge. Tootsie's, which opened in 1960, is the top dog on the Honky Tonk Highway. Country artists such as Kris Kristofferson and Willie Nelson played there when they were young.

NATIONAL ZOO AT GRASSMERE
3777 Nolensville Pike, Nashville, 615-833-1534
www.nashvillezoo.org
This is not just a zoo, but really more like an amusement park, it has so many things to do. You can visit the **CROFT HOME**, built in 1810—it's the centerpiece of the **GRASSMERE HISTORIC FARM** and is open seasonally for guided tours. Guides will take you on a walking tour through the home, telling you the history of the property, stories from the five generations who lived there, and how the Zoo came to be located on the land. During the tour, you will see many original pieces of furniture, a portion of the extensive book collection, and several family portraits. Be sure to look for the name that was etched on a pane of glass over 100 years ago. After touring the home, you can explore the rest of the farm grounds, including the three-tier heirloom garden and the family cemetery, which is the final resting place for several family members. You will really want

to see **THE CASSOWARY EXHIBIT**. The cassowary is a keystone species to Australia and New Guinea playing a vital role in the growth of the rainforest. Known as the Gardener of the Rainforest, cassowaries can germinate more than 200 species of plants, thus providing food for other species. **JUNGLE GYM** is the largest community-built playground in the United States. You can swing like a gibbon, run like the zebras and prowl around tiger-style in the 66,000-square foot playground. Jungle Gym features include: a 35-foot tall "Tree of Life" tree house structure; super slides, cargo netting and swings; a concrete sculpture garden, with a giant snake tunnel, bat cave, hippo and crocodile figures; dancing water fountain. **WILD ANIMAL CAROUSEL**. Visitors love taking rides on the 39 brightly-colored, wooden animals. The beautifully painted carousel features species found at the Zoo as well as several other exciting animals expected to arrive in the future. It is the first carousel in the country to offer the opportunity to ride a giant anteater or a clouded leopard cub.

OZ ARTS NASHVILLE
6172 Cockrill Bend Cir, Nashville, 615-350-7200
www.ozarts**nashville**.org
A new and unique destination for performing and visual art experiences. On-site eatery and bar.

ROLLER DERBY
Nashville Roller Girls
www.nashvillerollergirls.com
Nashville's only all-female, flat track roller derby league. They have 2 teams, with members separated by speed and skill level. Try to see the Music City All Stars—those girls are scary tough! Check out website for schedule and events listings.

RYMAN AUDITORIUM
116 Fifth Ave. N., Nashville, 615-889-3060
www.ryman.com
The "Mother Church of Country Music" was built in 1892 in what would become downtown Nashville by businessman Thomas G. Ryman as a venue for evangelist Sam Jones called the Union Gospel Tabernacle. (Don't you love that name?) From 1943-1974, it was the home of the Grand Ole Opry, the long-running, weekly radio showcase made up of a variety of big-name and smaller country acts.

A National Historic Landmark, the Ryman is open for tours. Costumes, programs and other memorabilia tied to performers such as Hank Williams, Minnie Pearl and Roy Acuff are prominently displayed on the first and second floors. The Ryman is also where Rayna (Britton) and Juliette (Panettiere) did the duet "Wrong Song" in the first season of the TV show "Nashville." Today, the Ryman only hosts the Grand Ole Opry between November and January. With the acoustics and the crescent arc to the pew seating, it's hard to find a bad seat. Depending on who's playing, tickets are sometimes available the day of the show. And you never know who will be playing.

TOMATO ART FEST
www.tomatoartfest.com

The Tomato Art Fest was founded by Meg and Bret MacFadyen, owners of East Nashville's Art and Invention Gallery. In 2004, the gallery hosted an art show celebrating the tomato in late summer, and planned a few neighborhood events to promote the show. The Tomato Art Fest proved so popular that it immediately turned into an annual, signature event for the hip, urban neighborhood of East Nashville. It's held in August.

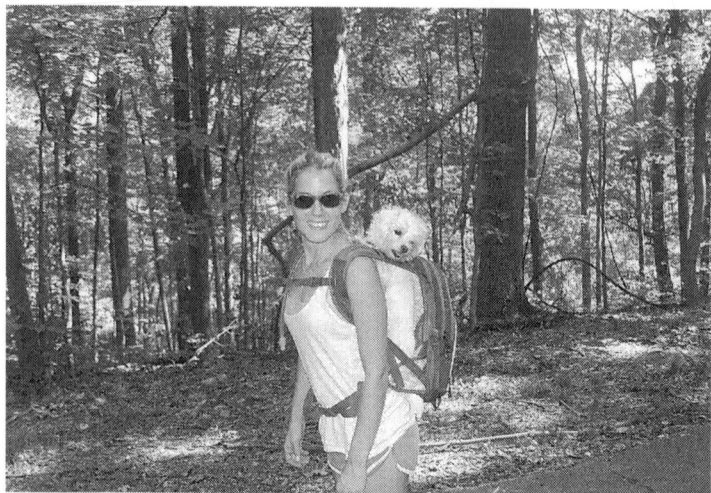

WARNER PARK NATURE CENTER
7311 Highway 100, Nashville, 615-352-6299
www.tnvacation.com/vendors/warner_park_nature_center
This park is huge, and there's always something going on here.
The Nature Center serves as a jumping-off point for exploring
the 2,600 acres of Nashville's Percy Warner and Edwin Warner
Parks. They have a wide range of environmental education
programs, school field trips, educator training workshops,
outdoor recreation programs and other special activities for
people of all ages. They also serve as a natural history and
education reference center for individuals and groups. They
promote and serve as a resource for organic gardening and
native plant landscaping. Their campus includes the **Susanne
Warner Bass Learning Center** which houses a natural history
museum and programming space; the **Milbrey Warner Waller
Library complete** with an extensive collection of natural history
titles; the **Emily Warner Dean Administration Building**; a
working organic garden including a greenhouse and a cedar
shade house; a wildflower garden and fern garden; the Frist
teaching pond; grounds landscaped with native plants; and the
main trailhead for twelve miles of hiking trails.

YAZOO BREWING COMPANY
910 Division St, Nashville, 615-891-4649
www.yazoobrew.com
NEIGHBORHOOD: Downtown; the Gulch
Though they went into business in 2003, as they expanded, they
ended up moving into this building in 2010 so they could
continue growing. Their taproom is open Wednesday through
Friday evenings from 4-8pm, as well as Saturdays from 12-6
pm, serving their full lineup of beers. They also offer sampler
trays so you can run the full gamut of their selections. You can
order cheese plates, chips & salsa, spiced pecans, and beer bread
- made with Yazoo of course. All food items are locally made,
locally grown. They offer a **WORKING BREWERY TOUR**,
but check their web site for the schedule.

Chapter 6
SHOPPING & SERVICES

THE ARCADE
244 5th Ave N, Nashville
www.nashvilledowntown.com/go/the-arcade
Located in the center of the downtown Nashville Arts District,
this historic shopping center hosts a variety of arts events.
Events include the Downtown Nashville **First Saturday Art
Crawl** (first Sat. of every month from 6 – 9 p.m.). Eateries are
on the first floor, with some of the best galleries in town (about

15 of them) located upstairs. Food venues include the **Peach Cobbler Factory, Phillyman, Manny's House of Pizza**, the **Peanut Shop** and the Uptown Branch of the United States Postal Service.

ART & INVENTION GALLERY

1106 Woodland St, Nashville, 615-226-2070
www.artandinvention.com
NEIGHBORHOOD: East Nashville
Before the Five Points District of East Nashville became a hip, fun destination, they saw its potential. With that vision in mind, Bret and Meg MacFadyen converted an old garage at 1106 Woodland Street in 2000 into an artist's studio, which they named the *Garage Mahal*. Three years later, the *Art & Invention Gallery* was born. Having five to six shows annually, including the signature Tomato Art Show in August and Holiday Artisan Show in December, *Art & Invention Gallery* focuses on inventiveness in fine art, craft and original furniture. Adult and Children Workshops are held throughout the year as an outlet for creative energy.

BILLY REID

4015 Hillsboro Pike, Nashville, 615-292-2111
www.billyreid.com
NEIGHBORHOOD: Green Hills
Check out the Southern-inspired, hipster classics on sale here for men and women—shoes, heirloom, bags, jackets, blazers, shirts, caps, chinos, denim, accessories, gifts, Tees, outerwear.

GOODBUY GIRLS

1108 Woodland St, Nashville, 615-281-9447
www.goodbuygirlsnashville.com
Clothing shop for women that features a mix of vintage and new clothing. It has about the best selection of cowboy boots you'll find naywhere, some with fringe, feathers, embroidery. (They are all used, or as we say now, "pre-worn.")

GRIMEY'S
1604 8th Ave S, Nashville, 615-254-4801
www.grimeys.com
No question this is the best indie record store in Nashville.

H. AUDREY
4027 Hillsboro Pike, Nashville, 615-760-5701
www.haudrey.com
NEIGHBORHOOD: Green Hills; Hill Center
The clothing scene has improved dramatically in recent years, a lot because of places like this one, which is run by Hank Williams's granddaughter, Holly. Rick Owens leather jackets, Haute Hippie, Rag & Bone and Helmut Lang—labels you expect to find in New York and L.A., but not here.

HILLSBORO VILLAGE
21st Ave, Nashville, No Phone
http://www.visitmusiccity.com/visitors/neighborhoods/hillsboro village
NEIGHBORHOOD: 21st & Vanderbilt, Hillsboro, West End
A good shopping area that runs along 21st Avenue just below Vanderbilt. Lots of interesting little shops located here.

HIP ZIPPER VINTAGE

1008 Forrest Ave, Nashville, 615-228-1942
www.hipzipper.com
NEIGHBORHOOD: East Nashville
A place for high quality, reasonable priced vintage clothing.
Nashville's oldest all-vintage clothing shop. They will buy
men's & women's vintage clothing and accessories from the
1930s to the 1980s. This includes (but isn't limited to) ladies'
dresses, lingerie, swimsuits, sweaters, hats, purses, shoes, boots,
eyeglasses, belts, jewelry, as well as men's suits, Western shirts,
denim, cardigans, jackets, bow ties, hats, eyeglasses belts and
more.

IMOGENE & WILLIE
2601 12th Ave S, Nashville, 615-292-5005
www.imogeneandwillie.com
NEIGHBORHOOD: 12 South, Belmont, Hillsboro
In what used to be an old gas station is a hot shop where it's all about the jeans, blue and otherwise. Painstaking craftsmanship. Their tattooed staff will tailor your purchase specifically for you (but you might have to wait a few days to take it home—or have them ship it.) Denim for the most discriminating buyer (which means it's expensive). Clothes for men and women; lots of good gift ideas, too, if you look at their accessories. Some one-of-a-kind items, including hats, jackets, textiles, distressed leather trench boots. Definitely a must stop for the shopaholic.

KATY K DESIGNS AT RANCH DRESSINGS
2407 12th Ave S, Nashville, 615-297-4242
www.katyk.com
NEIGHBORHOOD: 12 South, Belmont, Hillsboro
Country-western outfits are the name of the game here. The shop is well stocked with new and especially good *vintage* Western boots and shirts, hats, men's and women's clothing. A great variety of those Western shirts with embroidery all over the front and back. If you don't feel like a country-western singing star when you come out of here, you'll at least feel like a local.

LEONA
2309 12th Ave S, Nashville, 615-383-1293
www.leonany.com
NEIGHBORHOOD: Belmont / Hillsboro / 12 South
Lauren Leonard designs for such stars as Guiliana Rancic and
Taylor Swift, and now she has her own store featuring pocket
tees; tops, dresses, halters, long-sleeved Simon blouses; Bennett
jackets; bottoms; nice lacy swimsuits; some jewelry (sold gold
cuff; chunky chain necklaces; leather wrap bracelets; belts.

LOCAL HONEY
2009 Belmont Blvd, Nashville, 615-915-1354
http://www.lhnashville.com/
NEIGHBORHOOD: Belmont, Hillsboro
This is a hair salon that doubles as a clothing store offering
threads by local designers (as well as some vintage). I love this
store.

MOTEL SHOPS
THE LOVELESS CAFÉ
8400 Hwy 100, Nashville, 615-646-9700
www.lovelesscafe.com
Before the Loveless Café got so famous, the 14 rooms behind
the place were rented out like any other motel. Now they have
been converted into a series of privately owned shops that are a
lot of fun to visit. **Hams & Jams Country Store** is where you
can get not only the café's homemade preserves and country
hams, but also lot of gifts handmade by Tennessee artisans,
Loveless Café mugs and other merchandise and souvenirs.
Homemade pies and sweets. You can get their pit-smoked BBQ
here as well, by the pound or in a sandwich. (I've come in here
to get a sandwich when the waiting line was too long at the
café.) **Shimai Pottery & Gifts** has great gift items. In addition
to their paintings, sculpture and tableware, Shimai offers fine
handcrafted jewelry, textiles, shimmering hand-colored
photographs and exquisite carved wood. Features works from
some of the area's finest artisans. **Faithful Places** has timeless
antiques, books, home décor and accessories, gifts and unique
art objects.

NASHVILLE FARMERS' MARKET

900 Rosa Parks Blvd, Nashville, 615-880-2001
www.nashvillefarmersmarket.org
NEIGHBORHOOD: Downtown
The Farmers' Market in Nashville is really, really beautiful.
From the vendors in the covered space you can buy your
groceries, buy your vegetables and your plants, preserves and
jams, and then you can have something to eat at one of the little
indoor restaurants. The fish places are fantastic, too.

OLD MADE GOOD

3701B Gallatin Pike, Nashville, 615-432-2882
www.oldmadegoodnashville.com/
A vintage goods boutique offering everything from jewelry and
clothing to handmade art and furniture, some of it by local
artisans. This is one of the hipper stores in Nashville.

PANGAEA

1721 21st Ave S, Nashville, 615-269-9665
www.pangaeanashville.com
NEIGHBORHOOD: Hillsboro/West End, 21st/Vanderbilt
Opened in 1987 in a small and out-of-the-way space, featuring
vintage clothing and Guatemalan imports. Through 20 years and
two moves, Pangaea has become an anchor store in bustling

Hillsboro Village. Packed with women's and men's new clothing, silver jewelry from around the world, beautiful mirrors, lamps and linens, folk art from Mexico, books, toys and quirky gifts, it's hard to take it all in during one visit.

PEABODY SHOE REPAIR
718 Thompson Lane, Suite 105, Nashville, 615-292-5214
No Website
NEIGHBORHOOD: Hillsboro
There's a crusty old repairman in here who's worth the visit, but the reason I mention this place at all (since I don't expect you to take your shoes in here to get a shine) is that you can pick up a great pair of secondhand cowboy boots.

SAVANT VINTAGE
2302 12th Ave, Nashville, 615-385-0856
No Website
NEIGHBORHOOOD: 12 South, Belmont, Hillsboro

On the two floors of this big store you'll find a gargantuan selection of vintage items, from thousands of items of old clothing to shoes, furniture, accessories, you name it. Savant is known for being pricey (way pricey in some cases), but don't try to haggle with the owner. The prices are firm and she'll bite your neck off.

THIRD MAN RECORDS
623 7th Ave S, Nashville, 615-891-4393
www.thirdmanrecords.com
Open since 2009, this venue features a record store, record label offices, photo studio, dark room, and live venue. All records are recorded, printed and pressed in Nashville.

THOUSAND FACES
1720 21st Ave S, Nashville, 615) 298-3304
www.athousandfaces.com
NEIGHBORHOOD: Hillsboro/West End, 21st/Vanderbilt
A jumble of neat stuff for the gift giving connoisseur. Jewelry is a focal point with a selection not found on the beaten path. Pottery, glass, wood, metal, canvas and a great selection of cards are staples of this fun shop.

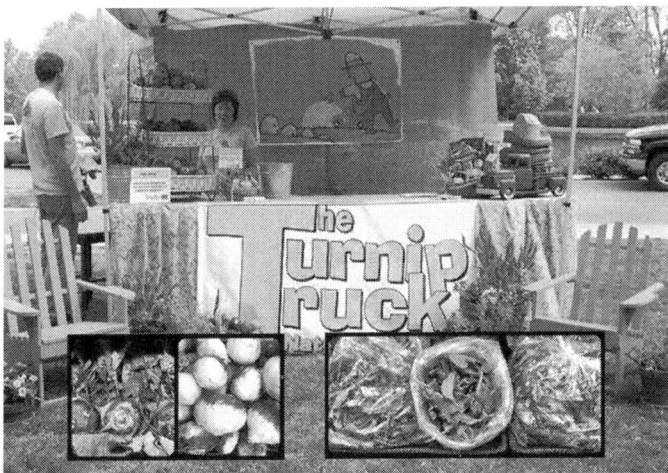

THE TURNIP TRUCK
The Turnip Truck Natural Market
970 Woodland St, Nashville, 615-650-3600
www.theturniptruck.com
NEIGHBORHOOD: Downtown, Gulch
More than just a wonderful health food market and store. One of the few places in town where you can get fresh juice made with organic produce. They use as much organic produce as we

can. Occasionally, depending on the season, it is cost prohibitive for them to have 100% organic but they'll gladly let you know on a day to day basis what is available. Here are some of their specialty blends: **The Doug Funny** has apples, lemon, carrots, beets, and ginger. **The Hulk** is made with cucumbers, kale, spinach, parsley, celery, apple, and lemon. **The Ninja Turtle** has celery, spinach, parsley, broccoli, and cucumber. **Mister Rogers** is a blend of carrots, apples, oranges, and celery.

UAL (United Apparel Liquidators)

2918 West End Ave, Nashville, 615-340-9999
www.shopual.com
Founded in 1980, this company now boasts 5 retail stores in 4 states. The store offers a great selection of high-end ladies' fashions at affordable prices. Think Chanel. Also carries overstocked item from nearby stores.

VENETIAN NAIL SPA

2114 Green Hills Village Drive, Nashville, 615-292-7727
www.venetiansalon.com
NEIGHBORHOOD: Green Hills
Nicole Kidman once got a manicure here when she was in town working on a movie. It's in the **Mall at Green Hills**, which has upscale stores like **Michael Kors** and **Louis Vuitton**, and is a great place for laid-back shopping and walking around.

INDEX

98

Other Books by the Same Author

Andrew Delaplaine has written in widely varied fields: screenplays, novels (adult and juvenile), travel writing, journalism. His books are available in quality bookstores as well as all online retailers.

Jack Houston
St. Clair Political Thrillers

The Keystone File – Part 1
The Keystone File – Part 2
The Keystone File – Part 3
The Keystone File – Part 4
The Keystone File – Part 5
The Keystone File – Part 6
The Keystone File – Part 7 (final)

On Election night, as China and Russia mass soldiers on their common border in preparation for war, there's a tie in the Electoral College that forces the decision for President into the House of Representatives as mandated by the Constitution. The

incumbent Republican President, working through his Aide for Congressional Liaison, uses the Keystone File, which contains dirt on every member of Congress, to blackmail members into supporting the Republican candidate. The action runs from Election Night in November to Inauguration Day on January 20. Jack Houston St. Clair runs a small detective agency in Miami. His father is Florida Governor Sam Houston St. Clair, the Republican candidate. While he tries to help his dad win the election, Jack also gets hired to follow up on some suspicious wire transfers involving drug smugglers, leading him to a sunken narco-sub off Key West that has $65 million in cash in its hull.

THE RUNNING MATE
A Jack Houston St. Clair Political Thriller

Sam Houston St. Clair has been President for four long years and right now he's bogged down in a nasty fight to be re-elected. A Secret Service agent protecting the opposing candidate discovers that the candidate is sleeping with someone he shouldn't be, and tells his lifelong friend, the President's son Jack, this vital information so Jack can pass it on to help his father win the election. The candidate's wife has also found out about the clandestine affair and plots to kill the lover if her husband wins the election. Jack goes to Washington, and becomes involved in an international whirlpool of intrigue.

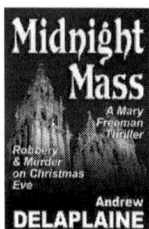

MARY FREEMAN SERIES
MIDNIGHT MASS - A Mary Freeman Thriller

Det. Lt. Mary Freeman stumbles upon a spectacular robbery of historic Trinity Church in downtown Manhattan on Christmas Eve, and after impressing the Mayor, gets assigned to the Task Force investigating the crime, throwing her headlong into a world of political intrigue and murder that rips apart every aspect of her life.

Jake Bricker Series

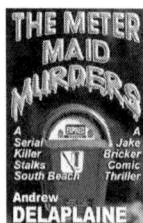

THE METER MAID MURDERS
A Jake Bricker Comic Thriller

102

A serial killer is loose on South Beach. But he's only killing meter maids, threatening the economic foundation of Miami Beach. Mayor Johnny Germane wants the killer caught NOW! But tall, dark and handsome Det. Sgt. Jake Bricker can't seem to nab the devious killer, even though he knows who the next victim will be. [Foul language; not for kids.]

The Adventures of Sherlock Holmes IV

In this series, the original Sherlock Holmes's great-great-great grandson solves crimes and mysteries in the present day, working out of the boutique hotel he owns on South Beach.

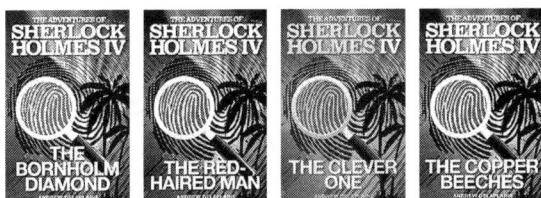

THE BORNHOLM DIAMOND

A mysterious Swedish nobleman requests a meeting to discuss a matter of such serious importance that it may threaten the line of succession in one of the oldest royal houses in Europe.

THE RED-HAIRED MAN

A man with a shock of red hair calls on Sherlock Holmes to solve the mystery of the Red-haired League.

THE CLEVER ONE

A former nun who, while still very devout, has renounced her vows so that she could "find a life, and possibly love, in the real world." She comes to Holmes in hopes that he can find out what happened to the man who promised to marry her, but mysteriously disappeared moments before their wedding.

THE COPPER BEECHES

A nanny reaches out to Sherlock Holmes seeking his advice on whether she should take a new position when her prospective employer has demanded that she cut her hair as part of the job.

THE MAN WITH THE TWISTED LIP

In what seems to be the case of a missing person, Sherlock Holmes navigates his way through a maze of perplexing clues that leads him through a sinister world to a surprising conclusion

THE DEVIL'S FOOT

Holmes's doctor orders him to take a short holiday in Key West, and while there, Holmes is called on to look into a case in which three people involved in a Santería ritual died with no explanation.

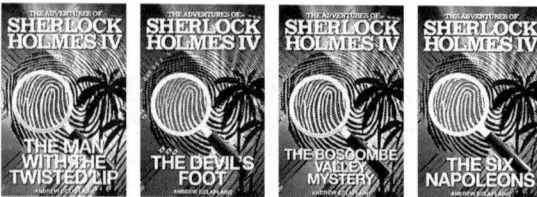

THE BOSCOMBE VALLEY MYSTERY

Sherlock Holmes and Watson are called to a remote area of Florida overlooking Lake Okeechobee to investigate a murder where all the evidence points to the victim's son as the killer. Holmes, however, is not so sure.

THE SIX NAPOLEONS

Inspector Lestrade calls on Holmes to help him figure out why a madman would go around Miami breaking into homes and businesses to destroy cheap busts of the French Emperor. It all seems very insignificant to Holmes—until, of course, a murder occurs.

The Trap Door Series

THE TRAP DOOR: THE "LOST" SCRIPT OF CARDENIO

A boy goes back to 1594 and Shakespeare's original Globe

Theatre in search of a "lost" play by the world's greatest writer, and ends up embroiled in the plot to kill Queen Elizabeth the First and replace her with Mary, Queen of Scots. [Highly suitable for kids.]

The Annals Of Santopia

SANTOPIA: PART I, BOOK 1
SANTA & THE LOST PRINCESS

Three days before Christmas in the year 1900, Connie Claus has a son, and Santa names the boy Nicholas. Ameritus, Great Sage of Santopia, issues a Prophecy – the next girl born in the Kingdom will grow up to become Prince Nicky's Queen, and Nicky will become betrothed to her on his eighteenth birthday when he is invested as the future Santa at the Ritual of the Green Gloves. Far across Frozen Lake, the Baroness von Drear gives birth to a baby girl – she's overjoyed that her new baby will be the future Queen of Santopia. But when she discovers another girl was born just hours before her own to Taraxa and Inula, peasant family living in her Realm, she sets out to destroy them.

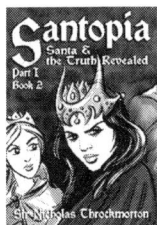

SANTOPIA: PART I, BOOK 2
SANTA & THE TRUTH REVEALED

It's Christmas Eve, and Elf Duncan journeys to the Other World as a stowaway on the Grand Sleigh. When discovered, he is forced to stay with the Red Elves in their Warren deep below the Tower of London until Santa can send a sleigh to bring him home. Back in Santopia during the same time period, Spicata rescues Taraxa and Inula from the carnivorous Pirandelves and gets them safely to Santopolis where he hopes to discover the real story behind the missing baby girl, thinking his reward would be great if he could get new information to the Baroness.

Screenplays

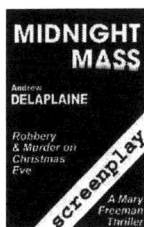

MIDNIGHT MASS – THE
SCREENPLAY

Det. Lt. Mary Freeman stumbles upon a spectacular

robbery of historic Trinity Church in downtown Manhattan on Christmas Eve, and after impressing the Mayor, gets assigned to the Task Force investigating the crime, throwing her headlong into a world of political intrigue and murder that rips apart every aspect of her life. (Based on the novel.)

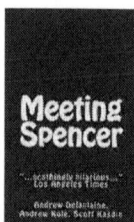

MEETING SPENCER – THE SCREENPLAY

After a series of Hollywood flops, famed director Harris Chappell (Jeffrey Tambor in the movie released in 2012) returns to New York to relaunch his Broadway career. But Chappell's triumphant comeback begins to spiral out of control into a wild night of comic misadventure after meeting struggling actor Spencer (Jesse Plemons) and his old flame Didi (Melinda McGraw). This is an original script (not based on a novel or other source material). This is the original script, NOT the shooting script. You can stream the movie on Netflix. Or buy it on Amazon.

THE TRAP DOOR – THE SCREENPLAY

Looking for a famous "lost" play, a London boy performing in "A Midsummer Night's Dream" travels back in time to 1594 and the original production of the play in the original Globe Theatre. While there, he becomes embroiled in a plot to assassinate the Protestant Queen Elizabeth the First and replace her with the Catholic Mary, Queen of Scots. (Based on the novel.)

Delaplaine Travel Guides

Delaplaine Travel Guides represent the author's take on some of the many cities he's visited and many of which he has called home (for months or even years) during a lifetime of travel. The books are available as either ebooks or as printed books. Owing to the ease with which material can be uploaded, **both the printed and ebook editions** are updated 3 times a year.

The Long Weekend Series

Annapolis
Appalachicola
Atlanta
Austin
Berlin
Beverly Hills
Birmingham
Boston
Brooklyn
Cancún (Mexico)
Cannes
Cape Cod
Charleston
Charlotte
Chicago
Clearwater – St. Petersburg
Coral Gables
El Paso
Fort Lauderdale
Fort Myers & Sanibel
Gettysburg
Hamptons, The
Hilton Head
Hollywood – West Hollywood
Hood River (Ore.)
Jacksonville
Key West & the Florida Keys
Lima (Peru)
London
Los Angeles / Downtown
Las Vegas
Louisville
Marseille
Martha's Vineyard
Memphis
Mérida (Mexico)
Mexico City
Miami & South Beach
Milwaukee
Myrtle Beach
Nantucket

Napa Valley
Naples & Marco Island
Nashville
New Orleans
New York / Brooklyn
Nee York / The Bronx
New York / Downtown
New York / Midtown
New York / Queens
New York / Upper East Side
New York / Upper West Side
Orlando & the Theme Parks
Palm Beach
Panama City (Fla.)
Paris
Pensacola
Philadelphia
Portland (Ore.)
Provincetown
Rio de Janeiro
San Francisco
San Juan
Santa Monica & Venice
Sarasota
Savannah
Seattle
Sonoma County
Tampa Bay
Venice (Calif.)
Washington, D.C.
West Hollywood & Hollywood

Made in the USA
Middletown, DE
06 December 2015